What Are the Skills Required to Obtain a Good Job?

An Analysis of Labor Markets, Occupational Features, and Skill Training for the Youth ChalleNGe Program

KATHRYN A. EDWARDS, MELANIE A. ZABER, DANIEL SCHWAM

Prepared for the Office of the Secretary of Defense
Approved for public release; distribution unlimited

NATIONAL DEFENSE RESEARCH INSTITUTE

For more information on this publication, visit **www.rand.org/t/RRA271-3**.

About RAND

The RAND Corporation is a research organization that develops solutions to public policy challenges to help make communities throughout the world safer and more secure, healthier and more prosperous. RAND is nonprofit, nonpartisan, and committed to the public interest. To learn more about RAND, visit www.rand.org.

Research Integrity

Our mission to help improve policy and decisionmaking through research and analysis is enabled through our core values of quality and objectivity and our unwavering commitment to the highest level of integrity and ethical behavior. To help ensure our research and analysis are rigorous, objective, and nonpartisan, we subject our research publications to a robust and exacting quality-assurance process; avoid both the appearance and reality of financial and other conflicts of interest through staff training, project screening, and a policy of mandatory disclosure; and pursue transparency in our research engagements through our commitment to the open publication of our research findings and recommendations, disclosure of the source of funding of published research, and policies to ensure intellectual independence. For more information, visit www.rand.org/about/principles.

RAND's publications do not necessarily reflect the opinions of its research clients and sponsors.

Published by the RAND Corporation, Santa Monica, Calif.
© 2022 RAND Corporation
RAND® is a registered trademark.

Library of Congress Cataloging-in-Publication Data is available for this publication.
ISBN: 978-1-9774-0856-3

Cover: Jon Soucy/U.S. National Guard.

Limited Print and Electronic Distribution Rights

About This Report

The National Guard Youth ChalleNGe (ChalleNGe) program is a residential, quasi-military program for youth ages 16 to 18 who are experiencing difficulty in traditional high school. The Office of the Assistant Secretary of Defense for Manpower and Reserve Affairs asked the RAND Corporation to develop a set of measures that focus on various aspects of ChalleNGe with an overall goal of improving program effectiveness. The RAND team's analyses of ChalleNGe began in September 2016. This report is part of that effort. It focuses on the job skills and investments that ChalleNGe sites can make part of their education curriculum, separate from starting up or participating in an occupational training program or credential program.

This report will be of greatest interest to ChalleNGe program staff and directors at individual sites and to program staff and directors at the six Job ChalleNGe sites. It will also be of interest to personnel providing oversight for the ChalleNGe program, staff at similarly targeted youth intervention programs, and policymakers concerned with labor market opportunities for workers without education beyond high school.

The research reported here was completed in July 2021 and underwent security review with the sponsor before public release.

RAND National Security Research Division

This research was sponsored by the Office of the Assistant Secretary of Defense for Manpower and Reserve Affairs and conducted within the Forces and Resources Policy Center of the RAND National Security Research Division (NSRD), which operates the National Defense Research Institute (NDRI), a federally funded research and development center sponsored by the Office of the Secretary of Defense, the Joint Staff, the Unified Combatant Commands, the Navy, the Marine Corps, the defense agencies, and the defense intelligence enterprise.

For more information on the RAND Forces and Resources Policy Center, see http://www.rand.org/nsrd/frp or contact the director (contact information is provided on the webpage).

Acknowledgments

The authors would like to thank Grace Gahlon and Nathan Edenfield for their research assistance. We are grateful for helpful comments and feedback from Andrew Green and Matt Baird.

Summary

In the U.S. labor market, which jobs workers can attain can be highly dependent on their education. This is often crudely divided into high-paying jobs (requiring at least a bachelor's degree) and low-paying jobs (requiring only a high school diploma or less). The so-called *middle-skills* pathway encompasses workers who have a high school diploma and additional, subbaccalaureate training (Carnevale et al., 2018).

The National Guard Youth Challenge Program (ChalleNGe) is in a unique position to provide occupational guidance and support to its participants. ChalleNGe is a federal-state partnership run through the National Guard. The ChalleNGe program began in the 1990s as a residential, quasi-military intervention program for high school dropouts age 16 to 18 that helped them prepare for or attain a General Educational Development (GED), the high school equivalency certificate. The program is located in participating states. Each program location, or site, is run through a state-federal partnership in conjunction with the National Guard.

Further characterization of ChalleNGe can be difficult, since sites vary from one another and evolve policy and practice over time. Today, ChalleNGe can no longer be described as a dropout or GED program, because many sites offer credit recovery (with the intention that program participants, called *cadets*, return to high school), and some are registered in high schools that offer traditional diplomas (Wenger, Constant, and Cottrell, 2018). However, all sites include a five-and-a-half-month residential stay, during which cadets spend their day in a combination of classroom instruction and physical activities, building their capabilities in many areas, including academic excellence, responsible citizenship, job skills, and life-coping skills. The cadets are organized in a quasi-military structure; they are typically assigned to a platoon, learn to march, and wear fatigues.

Given that cadets live in residence for five and a half months, ChalleNGe sites have, in theory, ample opportunity for investments in occupation-specific training to help cadets get on the path to successful careers. In practice, however, time is not the only factor in occupation-specific training. The costs of providing occupation-specific training can be prohibitive in terms of physical space, compensation of instructors, or credentialing fees. Further, selecting an occupation for investment is not without risk. Cadets arrive at ChalleNGe with a range of educational needs, measured either through their initial Test for Adult Basic Education score or the number of high school credits they have, both of which could also reflect varying ages of 16 to 18 (Wenger, Constant, and Cottrell, 2018). Cadets also come from a variety of labor markets within the state, some from outlying rural areas and some from urban centers. The varying traditional educational needs and home labor markets can render a specific occupational investment difficult for sites to make.

The goal of this report is to provide ChalleNGe administrators and site directors with insights into the labor market that cadets will enter and strategies ChalleNGe staff can use to better prepare cadets for it. We take a top-down, occupation-based approach to identifying training investments for cadets. Rather than trying to determine which occupation or set of occupations would make the "best" investment, we analyze labor market information on attainable, growth-oriented, high-paying middle-skills occupations to identify a *set of portable skills* that can help ChalleNGe participants succeed in any number of occupations or training programs. These skills form the basis for a set of investment recommendations for ChalleNGe.

We do this by first identifying a set of promising middle-skills occupations (*goal occupations*) for workers without a college degree, those meeting our criteria of being *attainable* (sufficient openings with limited entry requirements), *growth-oriented* (a career progression), and *high-paying* (above median wage). We then deconstruct those occupations into their core skills and determine which skills are shared across numerous occupations. This allows us to identify broad investments that sites can make to benefit all cadets (rather than just those in particular geographic areas or just those targeting a specific occupation) and remain affordable within the bounds of the program. There are five main steps in our approach:

1. Define what makes a job *good*, which will form our criteria for the goal occupations.
2. Identify the goal occupations.
3. Enumerate the skills of the goal occupations.
4. Synthesize the full set of skills into those most common among the goal occupations.
5. Summarize those common skills and how they can be acquired.

Key Findings

"Goal Occupations" for Cadets

We first sought to identify a set of promising middle-skills occupations, which we call *goal occupations* for workers without a college degree. These occupations had to meet our criteria of being attainable, growth-oriented, and high-paying.[1]

From the more than 800 U.S. occupations contained in the CPS data, we identified a total of 102 middle-skills goal occupations meeting our criteria of being attainable, growth-oriented, and high-paying. These occupations fell into two categories: (1) those from occupation families that require a mixed educational background (i.e., a high school diploma, post-secondary nondegree award, some college but no degree, or an associate degree), such as health care; and (2) those from occupation families that mostly or entirely do not require a college degree, such as production. The resulting list of goal occupations is not meant to be exhaustive, but it does provide an accessible group of occupations to study the job skills required for these occupations so that the ChalleNGe curriculum can be aligned to promote relevant skill development.

Skills, Knowledge, Abilities, and Work Environment Associated with the Goal Occupations

We analyzed the resultant goal occupations using the Occupational Information Network (O*NET), which describes the characteristics of more than 900 occupations in the United States. We identified nearly 50 characteristics or *elements* of the goal occupations that workers and experts in the O*NET had reported as being important to these occupations. These covered both capabilities (i.e., knowledge, skills, and abilities needed to perform a job) and the work environment (i.e., work activities, work styles, and work context that influence the nature of work and an individual's performance on the job). From the perspective of a ChalleNGe site director, both capabili-

---

[1] We conducted this analysis using the Current Population Survey (CPS; U.S. Census Bureau, U.S. Bureau of Labor Statistics, undated), and the Employment Projections (EP; U.S. Bureau of Labor Statistics, undated).

ties and environment represent areas of potential investment or training through in-class modules or other exercises.

Potential Investment Areas for ChalleNGe

We analyzed the list of common elements across the goal occupations, focusing on those that were important in performing an occupation and that aim at the medium skill level. Elements that were consistently ranked as important we compiled and used to produce a list of potential investments for ChalleNGe.

Many elements (whether a skill, an area of knowledge, an ability, or an environment) we identify as important to the goal occupations are already built into the ChalleNGe program. For example, math, English language, and reading comprehension are already part of the curriculum through classroom study. Others, such as interaction with computers or the ability to operate computers, could be integrated more. ChalleNGe also invests in training related to what O*NET calls *work styles*, i.e., traits that affect how well an individual performs a job. Work styles that are already built in to ChalleNGe training include initiative, independence, adaptability/flexibility, attention to detail, cooperation, dependability, integrity, self-control, stress tolerance, and persistence.

Skills in Which ChalleNGe Can Invest More

We identified six areas in which ChalleNGe might want to consider building on its investment. These areas are drawn from the potential investments listed above while grouping related skills together. Our goal in grouping them was not to find mutually exclusive categories but to think of how these elements might be brought into the ChalleNGe program.

Oral and Written Expression

Many of the important O*NET elements for the goal occupations center around oral and written communication and expression. Oral and written comprehension are important but are already included as part of the academic curriculum. Face-to-face discussions and communication over the telephone are common parts of many occupations. Workers are expected to express themselves clearly and effectively. The O*NET gives examples of these expression skills, such as writing a letter of recommendation, interviewing a job applicant, or giving directions to a lost driver. Simulations of these types of activities can be incorporated into the ChalleNGe classroom, into extracurricular activities, or into any opportunity for cadets to practice articulating their ideas clearly.

Being on and Communicating with a Team

Many of the goal occupations draw from fields in which teamwork and communication are important, from the construction site to the hospital room, and many of the O*NET elements reflect a team-based work environment. Important work activities include communicating with supervisors, peers, and subordinates. Daily work activities include working on a team and being in direct contact with others. One key skill is *active listening*, which involves giving full attention to what other people are saying, processing what they say, and not interrupting.

Cadets are organized in platoons and build group cooperation and dependability skills as part of the shared responsibility of good behavior, and the program includes an explicit emphasis on leadership and followership. However, cadets could benefit from broader opportunities to work or solve problems in small groups. This investment could occur in the classroom or as part of extracurricular activities and can also be complemented with small-team communication and practice.

Logic and Reasoning

Basic logic, reasoning, and problem solving are important to the performance of many occupations, as are critical thinking, complex problem solving, and inductive and deductive reasoning. Work-based examples of these skills and abilities include determining the prime suspect based on crime scene evidence, redesigning a floor layout of a workshop or plant to take advantage of new techniques, or knowing that a stalled car can roll downhill. There are many ways to incorporate logic games, puzzles—even mysteries or crime novels—into a cadet's repertoire while at ChalleNGe.

Information Expertise

While some of the goal occupations involve some hands-on physical labor, the focus of many others is on producing information. Capturing, ordering, processing, and remembering information are all key to many jobs. Important skills include *active learning*, which is defined as understanding the implications of new information. Important abilities include *information ordering*, or putting things or actions in a proper pattern or rule. Examples of information expertise include putting items in numerical order, assembling equipment based on instructions, following a blueprint, or making a budget. Further, important elements in work activities include getting information and documenting/recording information. ChalleNGe's academic focus can be seen as an investment in information expertise, but additional games or activities to encourage memory-building or pattern-recognition could be added.

Decisionmaking

Using information, facts, and data to make decisions is important to many of the goal occupations. This can involve evaluating information to make a decision, whether making a judgment or solving a problem, or weighing the costs and benefits of potential approaches in selecting a course of action. As adults navigating the world, cadets will have to make decisions regularly in their daily lives. As workers, this can require a coordinated effort. Decisionmaking spans deciding the menu at a cafeteria, selecting the location of a store, deciding how a break will affect worker productivity, or evaluating a loan application for risk. Advice and experience are the biggest aids for making life decisions and judgments, but professional decisionmaking and judgment are a matter of learning how to weigh potential actions and information. Judgment and decisionmaking can be incorporated into ChalleNGe through role playing, games, stories, and book discussion, among other activities.

Computer Familiarity

The use and knowledge of computers is important to many goal occupations. The decision to incorporate technology into cadets' education can be a function of budget and resources, or of overall approach. Many sites choose to incorporate technology or computers in only a minimal way, as they feel that cadets will not always use technology in accordance with the rules and that firewalls or website blocks can be worked around. While this is a valid concern, cadets also need to be fluent with computers for many jobs and may not come from the income backgrounds to have sufficient exposure to computers and opportunities to practice at home. In particular, cadets need to learn proper and professional communication skills and apply them in the appropriate setting, such as how to email a supervisor or how to follow up after a job interview.

Implications for Job ChalleNGe

Job ChalleNGe is a five-and-a-half-month residential program available to ChalleNGe graduates in some states. While the program emphasizes the same core components as ChalleNGe, the central focus of Job ChalleNGe is on occupational training. The information in this report can be useful to Job ChalleNGe staff in two ways. First, this report includes an exhaustive list of accessible jobs with good potential in terms of wages and growth (Appendix A includes the results using data from across the United States; Appendix B includes similar results while also documenting regional variation). This information may be helpful to program staff as they choose among available types of training (Job ChalleNGe training typically occurs through partnerships with local community colleges, where participants take training across a variety of fields; see Constant et al., 2020). But beyond training within specific fields, this report documents a list of skills that will be valuable for Job ChalleNGe graduates across a wide variety of jobs and occupations. These skills constitute a guide for Job ChalleNGe sites as they determine appropriate activities for their participants.

Conclusion

The skill investments that we recommend ChalleNGe site leaders incorporate into their programs and curricula should be good labor market investments, given their importance to attainable, growth-oriented, high-paying jobs. We do not discount the importance of specific credentials, such as a high school diploma, GED certificate, certification in food handling, or training as a certified nursing assistant. The skills and traits we document here do not have any commonly recognized credential, but their pervasive presence across many different occupations and industries indicates that these skills and traits will help cadets and Job ChalleNGe participants succeed in a challenging and often changing labor market. This research indicates that the work that program staff do to build these skills and traits will help to ensure cadets and Job ChalleNGe participants succeed and that the ChalleNGe program accomplishes its overall mission.

Contents

Figures, Tables, and List

Figures

Tables

List

The "Middle Skills" Pathway to Good Jobs—High-Paying Jobs That Do Not Require a College Degree

High school–educated workers without a college degree often have limited prospects in finding a "good" job that is high-quality and well compensated. To get on the path to a successful career, these graduates will likely need additional education or training, short of a bachelor's degree. One means of supplying this need is the *middle-skills* pathway, which encompasses workers who have a high school diploma and additional, subbaccalaureate training (Carnevale et al., 2018). The demand for workers with such training is growing, although acquiring those middle skills is not straightforward: There is incredible variation in the types of credentials a worker can get, where they can be obtained, how much they are valued in the labor market, and how long that value will last. And of course, the training itself may be quite expensive, both in direct costs of enrollment and indirect costs of missed paid employment time.

The National Guard Youth Challenge Program (ChalleNGe) is in a unique position to provide occupational guidance and support to its cadets, who spend five and a half months in a residential program with lots of classroom instruction. ChalleNGe is a multifaceted program that intervenes in the lives of young people age 16 to 18 who have dropped out or opted out of traditional high school. ChalleNGe is already making investments in helping cadets become productive citizens. The educational goal of ChalleNGe is to help cadets complete high school, whether through earning a GED or credit recovery. But academic education is only one part of ChalleNGe's eight core components: academic excellence, physical fitness, leadership/followership, responsible citizenship, job skills, service to community, health and hygiene, and life-coping skills.

During the residential portion of the ChalleNGe program, cadets spend ample time in the classroom, participating in scheduled activities and studying. Hence, they are a captive audience for skill investments. Yet, providing a new occupational training class, outfitting a separate classroom, or hiring an additional instructor to respond to changes in labor market demand can be beyond the budget for ChalleNGe administrators. Further, selecting an occupation for investment is not straightforward and not without risks. As it is, it is very difficult for sites to offer job training to all of their cadets in a cost-effective way, even aside from the difficulty of picking out what to offer, or knowing that the particular training is a worthwhile investment.

Options for Skills Investments

The goal of this report is to provide ChalleNGe administrators and site directors with insights into the labor market that cadets will enter and strategies ChalleNGe staff can use to better prepare cadets for it. Ultimately, the recommendations of this report will inform curriculum. There are two primary ways to align the curriculum with labor market needs—first, to identify a few promising occupations and develop curriculum to prepare cadets for those occupations specifically; second, to select a broader range of promising occupations and base the curriculum on elements common to that range.

The first approach has the benefit of clear pipelines. Selecting a single or select number of occupations, such as (concrete) flatwork finisher or HVAC installer, would allow ChalleNGe to issue an industry-recognized credential to cadets completing their training. It also would allow ChalleNGe sites to forge partnerships with local schools, employers, or trade associations to facilitate employment, apprenticeships, and job-based learning more broadly. Those partnerships would help employers to hire certified ChalleNGe graduates upon completion, with full knowledge of the extent of their training due to close collaboration.

There are some risks to betting on a single occupation (or even a narrow set). As noted in Appendix B, the vibrancy of the labor market for any one occupation can vary greatly by state and region. ChalleNGe sites are often distanced from cadets' homes; some cadets may come from close by, but others can come from farther away in the state. Cadets return home at the end of the residential phase to rural areas and urban centers that could be hundreds of miles apart. For many sites, however, an issue in investing in occupation-specific skills is cost and capacity. The physical site may not have sufficient classroom space or instructors for occupational training. In addition, not all cadets have the ability to take on additional training. Cadets vary in their educational needs when they arrive, ranging from those with very low initial Test of Adult Basic Education (TABE) scores and few high school credits to those who test at higher TABE levels and are just a few credits shy of finishing high school. In other words, some cadets have more room for extended nonacademic instruction (such as a training course) than others.

In this report, we take the second approach to identifying training investments for cadets. Rather than trying to determine which occupation or set of occupations would make the "best" investment, we focus instead on identifying a set of portable skills that can help ChalleNGe participants succeed in any number of occupations or training programs. By generalizing back to common skills, ChalleNGe can increase participants' employability while saving specific skill investments for employers. Many of the investments we identify can be incorporated into the existing curriculum and are therefore less costly. In addition, because they are not a full course, these investments can be made in all cadets, not solely those with sufficient additional academic time.

There are risks to this approach as well. A broader set of skills is less easily advertised to an employer, and without a narrow set of occupations, partnerships with employers are more challenging to arrange. However, the investment we identify should not be seen as incompatible with occupation-specific training, or as a substitute for it, but rather as a complement. A broader skill base is likely to serve cadets in their careers for a longer time, which is appropriate for young adults just entering the labor market.

Focus of This Report

We first identify a set of promising middle-skills occupations for workers without a bachelor's degree: those meeting our three criteria of being attainable, growth-oriented, and high-paying. We call these the *goal occupations*. We then deconstruct those occupations into their core skills and determine which skills are shared across numerous goal occupations. This allows us to identify broad investments that sites can make to benefit all cadets and remain affordable within the bounds of the program. There are five main steps in our approach:

1. Define what makes a job *good*, which will form our criteria for the goal occupations.
2. Identify the goal occupations.
3. Enumerate the skills of the goal occupations.
4. Synthesize the full set of skills into those most common among the goal occupations.
5. Summarize those common skills from an education perspective.

We explain this approach in detail in Chapter Three. In the remainder of this chapter, we delve further into the motivation for this study by describing the existing landscape of middle-skills training, including both its opportunities and its challenges, and we discuss the implications for ChalleNGe.

The Middle-Skills Pathway to Higher Earnings

On average, high school graduates do not earn as much as bachelor's degree holders. In 2018, the average hourly wage for high school graduates was $18.45, compared with $33.36 for four-year college graduates without an advanced degree (Gould, 2020). An average, of course, considers the earnings of all workers, young and old, and can reflect differences in the composition of the two groups. But even taking into account one dimension of compositional difference by focusing solely on younger workers, the difference between having a high school diploma or bachelor's degree is pronounced. In 2018, the median annual earnings for full-time, full-year high school graduates age 25 to 34 was $34,900, compared with $54,700 for full-time, full-year baccalaureate workers age 25 to 34 without an advanced degree (Annual Reports and Information Staff, Institute of Education Sciences, 2020). In both comparisons, high school graduates earn around 60 percent as much as bachelor's degree holders.

However, not all college graduates earn more than all high school graduates. Both sets of workers have a distribution in wages, and there is overlap across the incomes of college graduates and nongraduates. In Figure 1.1, we show the weekly earnings of five sets of workers in 2020 marked by their final educational attainment: less than high school, high school, some college or associate degree, bachelor's degree, and advanced degree. For each group, we show the earnings at different points of the wage distribution: the 10th percentile, which is the highest wage of the lowest 10 percent of earners within that group; the 25th, 50th (or median), 75th, and 90th percentile. At similar comparative points—such as comparing the 10th percentile of two groups—more education is associated with higher earnings. The 10th

FIGURE 1.1

Percentile Distribution of Weekly Earnings, by Educational Attainment, 2020

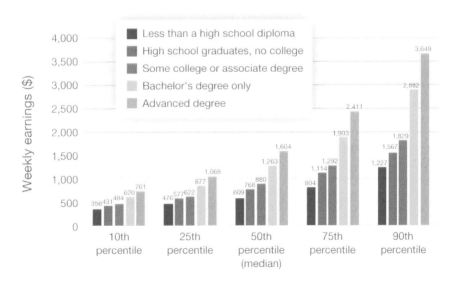

SOURCE: U.S. Bureau of Labor Statistics, 2020b, Table 5.

percentile for high school dropouts earn $356 a week, compared with $431 for high school graduates, $484 for some college, $620 for bachelor's degree holders, and $761 for advanced degrees. However, the distributions overlap. The 75th percentile high school graduate, for example, earns $1,114 a week, which is almost as much as the 50th percentile bachelor's degree holders, at $1,263, and higher than the 25th or 10th percentile for bachelor's degree holders, who earn $877 and $620, respectively.

The earnings distributions summarized in Figure 1.1 show, first, that the labor market rewards more education but, second, that college is not the only way to earn more. High school graduates can earn as much as college graduates. The challenge for high school graduates is to actually find and qualify for those high-paying jobs, a task which has only grown in difficulty over time (Carnevale et al., 2018).

However, the middle-skills pathway provides another potential means of getting a good job. Depending on sources, as much as a third of the workforce was estimated to be middle-skilled in 2012 (Modestino, 2016), and an estimated half of jobs in the labor market require middle-skills training (National Skills Coalition, undated-a, undated-b). Further, it is widely suggested that there is a shortage of middle-skilled workers (Kochan, Finegold, and Osterman, 2012; Holzer and Lerman, 2007; Harvard Business School, 2014; National Skills Coalition, undated-a).

The well-documented linkages between educational attainment and higher wages extend to subbaccalaureate training. In many surveys, workers without a four-year degree but more than a high school education are lumped together, as they are by the Bureau of Labor Statistics (BLS) in Figure 1.1, so that this group spans college dropouts in addition to associate degree holders and completers of vocational programs, whether they are credentialed or not—or whatever type of credential they have. As a group, their earnings are slightly higher than those for individuals with just a high school education. However, research into the returns of occupation-relevant credentials have found that having a credential is associated with higher earnings, although there is more evidence for licenses (Kleiner and Krueger, 2013; Gittleman, Klee, and Kleiner, 2018) than for certifications (Albert, 2017), and there is important variation by gender (Baird, Bozick, and Zaber, 2021).

The overall narrative is compelling: A traditional path to a high-paying job in the industrial economy through a high school diploma is closing, but middle-skills positions are accessible to high school graduates and in demand in the economy. However, in practice, the middle-skills path is not always straightforward or assured.

A Diversity of Programs and Credentials Constitute the Middle-Skills Pathway

One of the challenges of middle-skills educational pathways or middle-skills jobs is that the concept of *middle-skills*, whether describing the worker or the job, does not point to one specific level of educational attainment, or one agreed upon definition. The diversity of credentials associated with middle skills makes it difficult to describe, count, or predict the need for middle-skilled workers. Moreover, academic discussion of middle-skills jobs often focuses on questions of polarization and the well-being of those "moved" from the middle to the bottom (e.g., Oesch and Piccitto, 2019), rather than concretely identifying occupations within this band. For simplicity, we employ a middle-skills definition based on a range of educational attainment: education beyond a high school diploma, but no baccalaureate.

In Table 1.1, we present the array of subbaccalaureate credentials and what they require or signify. *Associate degrees* and *apprenticeship certificates* are nationally recognized. *Occupational licenses* vary in whether they are regulated by the federal, state, or local government but have the effect of limiting practitioners to those with a license and limiting those with a license to persons who meet some minimum education, training, and performance or proficiency standard. *Occupational certifications*, on the other hand, are often not required for employment but can signal qualifications or standards within an industry or group of practitioners. *Course certificates* indicate the completion of some type of training but do not necessarily signify competency.

These credentials are not only unequal in their benefit—licenses are associated with a higher wage bump than are other credentials, for example—but they are also not uniform in their use. Localities can differ in credential requirements, whether those requirements are issued by government or nongovernment agencies.

In addition, credentials vary not only by type, but also by quality. The U.S. Department of Labor (DoL), Employment and Training Administra-

TABLE 1.1

Subbaccalaureate Credentials in the United States

Credential	Issuer	Requirements and Significance
Associate degree (A.A.)	Accredited community or junior college	Two years of coursework
Apprenticeship certification, either completion or interim	DoL or State Apprenticeship Agency	Within a registered apprenticeship that meets qualification standards, the individual has met interim or final classroom and employment requirements.
Occupational license	Federal, state, or local government agency	Licenses are mandatory to practice certain occupations and are used to set professional standards within a market; they typically require a fee and proof of education or training.
Occupational certification, also known as personnel certification	Third-party nongovernmental agencies, such as industry associations	Are intended to set professional standards, as defined by an industry or group, rather than a government; typically requires completion of education, passage of an exam, and sometimes minimum amount of worker experience
Professional course certificate	Course provider	Demonstrates completion of a course or meeting, showing knowledge but not necessarily competency

SOURCE: DoL, Employment and Training Administration, 2010.

tion identifies four features of credential programs that indicate high quality and high potential for return on wage (DoL, Employment and Training Administration, 2010):

- **industry-recognized:** The credential is developed, offered, or endorsed by an industry association that represents a sizable portion of the industry.
- **stackable:** The credential is one in a sequence that can be accumulated over time to build up a worker's qualifications.

- **portable:** The credential is recognized in other geographies, institutions, industries, or companies.
- **accredited:** The credential comes from an educational institution that is accredited.

Education credentials offer an excellent example of a credential that exhibits all four features. The issuing of diplomas is regulated through the school accreditation process. Education credentials are often stackable—from high school diploma to A.A., B.A., to a professional or doctorate degree—and these degrees are recognized in all states and understood across all employers and industries.

Many occupational credentials, on the other hand, do not exhibit all four features. For example, the industry can have fractured certification norms, as is the case in information technology, an industry that has hundreds of credentials, with providers often competing with each other for share of the credential market (Credential Finder, undated). Or, a credential might not be accepted or recognized in another state, as is sometimes the case with licenses. In addition, the stackability of credentials requires coordination across the full credential path, but industry certifications and certificates are offered in a mostly disconnected or piecemeal fashion outside of the Title IV system.

Many Types of Institutions Offer Middle-Skills Education and Training

There is not room in this report to describe the full extent of middle-skills education in the United States, in particular because there are so many diffuse pathways within the overarching bucket of *middle skills*, which covers all postsecondary education and training below the baccalaureate level. Instead, we provide an overview of relevant institutions and legislation and describe some key concerns.

Community College System

The backbone of middle-skills education in the United States is the community college system, which offers a mix of courses for associate degrees, transfers to four-year colleges, educational certificates, and noncredit certificates. As an entity, the community college system was proposed by President Truman's Commission on Higher Education in 1947 as an expansion of the mix of private and public two-year junior colleges that existed at the time. Community colleges were intended to be universally accessible and to serve the diverse education needs of the community. The first public systems began in the 1950s and expanded through the 1960s and 1970s as all postsecondary enrollment grew with the large Baby Boomer generation (Ricketts, 2009).

Dropout rates at community colleges are high. In fact, fewer than half of all community college students have completed a degree or certificate after five years, and this effect is most pronounced among minority and low-income students (Bailey, Jenkins, and Leinbach, 2005). In addition, individuals from minority or low-income communities are more likely to be enrolled in remedial classes that are separate from classes with potential relevant occupational training (Holzer, 2011).

For-Profit Colleges and Schools

Offering subbaccalaureate education alongside the public community college system are for-profit colleges and schools. Depending on time and region, these for-profits have been known as proprietary schools, trade schools, career schools or career colleges, technical schools, and vocational schools. Traditionally, their educational programs were generally closely aligned to local labor demand, and most still offer career-oriented credential programs (Bailey, Badway, and Gumport, 2001). They existed for decades outside strict regulation and accreditation. These schools were brought under stricter regulation by congressional action in 1992 (Bailey, Badway, and Gumport, 2001), when the success of the University of Phoenix model led to a proliferation of for-profit colleges. Since then, they have grown in number and enrollment, and student eligibility for federal aid, such as Pell Grants and GI Bill funding, has fueled both dimensions of growth (Cellini, 2010). The quality of for-profit centers of instruction is a perennial concern, however. Research has consistently found that the earnings of for-profit graduates are lower than those of graduates from nonprofit schools (Deming, Goldin, and Katz, 2012; Liu and Belfield, 2014a; Liu and Belfield, 2014b, Cellini and Chaudhary, 2014).

Federal Programs

There are also federal programs that provide or subsidize middle-skills training. The Workforce Innovation and Opportunity Act (WIOA), a reauthorization of the Workforce Investment Act of 1998 (Pub. L. 105-220, 1998), was signed into law in 2014 to bolster the workforce development system. WIOA supports workers by funding postsecondary training programs. WIOA mandates that state labor agencies must provide an eligible training provider list so that prospective workers can research career and training options. In addition, training programs covered by WIOA receive significant funding from the fedcral government: In 2016, the federal government provided nearly $7 billion to states for core WIOA programs, including Adult Services, Dislocated Workers, Youth Services, Wagner-Peyser (a nationwide system of employment services), Adult Education and Literacy, and Rehabilitation Services. WIOA is predicated on the idea that the acquisition of a postsecondary credential is essential for forwarding long-term career prospects.

Industry Training

Finally, there is industry-provided training or industry-backed training. These programs can take many forms, as firms or industry associations can partner with local colleges to develop a curriculum or course, develop their own school or training, or provide scholarships to specific schools for training. These programs may be targeted at those new to the field or as professional development for continuing employees. Unions and guilds may also provide training for workers who are admitted as members, including those who are pursuing formal apprenticeship. Apprenticeships also occur outside unions and guilds—they are particularly common in the construction industry, which is a key source of middle-skills jobs. The DoL formalizes many programs as Registered Apprenticeship Programs; until recently, industry employers could also create paid Industry-Recognized Apprenticeship Programs, which were required to be paid and end in an industry-recognized credential (The White House, 2021).

Middle-Skills Training and Education Can Lead to Varied Labor Market Outcomes

Similar to the range in type, quality, and provision of middle-skills training and education programs, there is a range in the value of these programs in terms of job security and higher wages. The distribution of wages associated with levels of education, shown in Figure 1.1, demonstrates that middle-skills investments—from training programs to associate degrees and partial college attendance—correspond to a wide range of wages. At every point of comparison, whether median to median or 90th percentile to 90th percentile, those with some postsecondary education earn more than those with a high school diploma only. However, the difference is small in the bottom half: Compared with those with some postsecondary education, high school graduates earn $53 less per week at the 10th percentile, $45 less at the 25th, and $112 at the median.

As a result of the variation in wages associated with middle-skills training, individuals might invest in a middle-skills training program and not be better off as a result of it (indeed, with time out of the labor market, they may be worse off). We will not evaluate here differences in the training program quality or reputability. Assuming that an individual receives high-quality training and a credential, there are still several risks to the middle-skills investment.

Compensation

The first risk is related to compensation: A worker can complete a job-training program and then still make relatively low wages on the job. For example, 80 percent of hairdressers, hair stylists, and cosmetologists in the United States report that their job requires a postsecondary certificate, but the median annual earnings are only around $26,000, or $12.50/hour wage for a full-time, full-year worker (O*NET OnLine, 39-5012, undated-d).[1] In comparison, only 20 percent of home health aides (O*NET OnLine, 31-1121, 2021b) and almost no personal care aides (O*NET OnLine, 31-1122, 2021c)

---

[1]   The O*NET OnLine is a career information website that is sponsored by the DoL Employment and Training Administration. For each occupation we discuss, we cite the six-digit occupation code in O*NET that we used for the wage and education information listed. O*NET is discussed further in Chapter Two.

report that a postsecondary certificate is required, but the median earnings are still around $25,000. It could be that workers with a certificate earn more in those aide occupations than those who do not have a certificate, but the average pay is still relatively low and very similar to that in the beauty occupations, which do require more training. Just because a job requires training does not mean that it pays well.

Longevity

The second risk to middle-skills investment is longevity; a worker can complete a job-training program, but the skills learned can become less demanded over time, or even obsolete. For example, electronic home entertainment equipment installers and repairers (O*NET OnLine, 49-2097, 2020) earn around $40,000 annually, and around two-thirds report that their job requires a certificate. However, many of the certificates and skills that those jobs encompass have changed over time, as videocassette recorders, analog antennas, and televisions with cathode ray tube technology were replaced by liquid crystal displays and digital antennas. In addition to the threat of decreased demand or obsolescence, there is also a risk that trained skills would reduce in uniqueness or market power over time. In previous eras, an individual could become certified in typing at one of many secretarial schools in the United States, for example. Today, rather than being a unique skill that requires training, typing is now a core competency taught in high schools.

Availability

The third risk to middle-skills investment is availability; a worker can complete a job-training program, but the jobs can still be hard to come by. This can occur not only because the job is becoming rarer in the economy overall but also because the job is geographically concentrated or is prone to be cyclical.

For example, camera operators for television, video, and motion picture require at least an associate degree and have median earnings of $55,000 annually (O*NET OnLine, 27-4031, 2021a). However, nearly a third of the total jobs for this occupation are in California. Indeed, there are 8,300 camera operators in California but only 1,030 in Florida, despite Florida having half the population that California does.

Employers Have Diverse Expectations for Middle-Skilled Workers

Given that middle-skills training and education includes all subbaccalaureate occupation and vocational training, it is tempting to assume that the expectations for middle-skilled workers are limited to a technical need, defined by their training. However, the National Academies of Science, Engineering, and Medicine, in assessing the education system in the United States, found that workers in the United States need so-called "21st Century Skills" (National Research Council, 2011). These skills include information synthesis, creativity, problem-solving, communication, teamwork, and self-management. In general, the skills are oriented in inter- and intrapersonal competencies.

These skills are not new, but the concept of *21st-century skills* reflects the increased attention and demand for these in the current labor market, which reflects changes in the economy and labor market. Since 1970, the scope of U.S. jobs has increasingly shifted away from manual tasks and routine cognitive tasks to nonroutine cognitive tasks, such as problem-solving (Autor, Levy, and Murnane, 2003). Indeed, the National Academies notes that its assessment of skills is based on what employers report that they need from their workers. Researchers have found that people skills, such as communications, are an especially important factor in occupational and wage outcomes (Borghans, ter Weel, and Weinberg, 2008).

The National Academies is not the only research institution that has emphasized the importance of 21st-century skills, which have also been described as the seven "survival skills" (Wagner, 2008):

- critical thinking and problem solving
- collaboration and leadership
- agility and adaptation
- initiative and entrepreneurism
- effective oral and written communication
- assessing and analyzing information
- curiosity and imagination.

More broadly, these skills are characterized as "higher-order thinking" or "deeper learning outcomes" (Saavedra and Opfer, 2012). Critically, these

21st-century skills are needed by *all* workers, not just those with college or more education. Employers expect that even a worker with a technical certificate should have a minimal competency in these 21st-century skills.

Implications for ChalleNGe

The mission of ChalleNGe is to intervene in and reclaim the lives of at-risk youth to produce program graduates with the values, skills, education and self-discipline necessary to succeed as adults. Many ChalleNGe sites recognize that putting cadets on an upward trajectory will require more than high school equivalency or a diploma and are exploring how to incorporate job skills training into the residential period (Constant et. al., 2020). The changing landscape of middle-skills employment complicates the inclusion of job training. In addition, there are three key issues with incorporating jobs training into the residential phase of ChalleNGe.

First, the primary academic focus for cadets must be their high school education. Not only was this the original intention of the program, but even for sites that would like to incorporate more job training, many training programs require a high school diploma or equivalent. Most cadets had fallen behind before leaving traditional high school, and many will finish ChalleNGe without their GED or diploma in hand, despite having made considerable progress while on site. But the opposite is also true: Many cadets also complete their GED or diploma with ample time left in the program. This means that sites wanting to incorporate job training have to accommodate different academic capacity of the cadets as well as varying availability of the cadets for additional, nonacademic classroom time.

Second, sites are mostly resource-constrained in terms of physical, human, and monetary capital. Job training may require a separate classroom or may require equipment that needs to be purchased or rented. Space is not always freely available or costless to occupy at many ChalleNGe programs, and few have an excess of discretionary money that can be spent on equipment. And whatever the space or equipment requirements, job training requires instruction. Having a teacher on staff who can teach a job training class or a teacher who can be hired is not trivial. Hence, standing up job training on site can be difficult or impossible for ChalleNGe.

Third, partnership with local community colleges or career schools can be difficult. Several ChalleNGe sites have partnered with local institutions to send a small number of cadets for introductory job training. This can present logistical difficulties—such as transport—and also requires selecting which cadets get to participate and allowing cadets to have non-ChalleNGe instruction. The latter point can be problematic. Cadets are not typical high school or community college students; they are dressed in uniform, they have struggled with academics previously, and many have issues with authority and discipline. Site directors who partner with community colleges for job training have acknowledged that the cadets are treated differently, often worse, at the partnering institution. Instructors there can be resentful of having cadets in their class, whom they perceive to be of lower caliber than the "usual" students. In addition, this approach allows for job training to be given to only a limited number of cadets.

Job ChalleNGe is a five-and-a-half-month residential program that is available to ChalleNGe graduates in some states. Job ChalleNGe programs also face limitations, but in these programs the provision of job training takes on a central role. Training is provided by partners, generally local community colleges. But sites still may struggle to determine the most appropriate training programs for participants.

In short, offering cost-effective job training is difficult for ChalleNGe sites, and the difficulties are broader than the problems inherent in choosing the training to offer, or knowing that the particular training is a worthwhile investment. While Job ChalleNGe sites face somewhat different limitations, offering cost-effective training is a goal of these sites as well. This difficulty is the central motivation for this research report—how can a budget-constrained program make a job training investment for students with a range of academic abilities?

Organization of This Report

In the following chapters, we describe existing efforts to identify good occupations and then present our top-down, occupation-based approach to identifying occupational training investments for cadets. We hope to provide ChalleNGe administrators and site directors with options for broad investments that sites can make that benefit all cadets while ensuring that these efforts remain affordable within the bounds of the program.

The remainder of the report consists of five chapters. In Chapter Two, we discuss existing methods of identifying good occupations, which we compare with our own method of defining goal occupations. In Chapter Three, we discuss our methods and data sources for identifying good occupations and determining the common skills that can support cadets on their career pathways. In Chapter Four, we list and describe the goal occupations produced through our analysis, while in Chapter Five, we break down the skills and features of these occupations. In Chapter Six, we discuss the implications of the goal occupations and their common skills, providing recommendations for potential investments to support affordable occupational training through ChalleNGe programs.

CHAPTER TWO

What Is a Good Job? Part 1—How Good Jobs Are Identified in Existing Sources

In this chapter, we review three key sources of labor market information that are oriented to job seekers and new workers and compare their recommendations and assess their utility for informing ChalleNGe sites about broad-based middle-skills training investments. We consider the advantages and disadvantages of these current approaches to identifying subbaccalaureate occupations. The discussion in this chapter will help to inform our approach to identifying goal occupations, which we describe in Chapter Three.

We describe three sources of labor statistics. The first source is the Employment Projections (EP), which is produced by the BLS. The second source is labor market information (LMI), which is produced by state governments in accordance with WIOA and sponsored by DoL. The final source is a set of annual job prospects lists, published by private firms, which are often characterized as "fastest growing jobs" or the "hottest jobs" or something similar. All three sources have the goal of identifying occupations that would be good for job seekers and new workers because they are in demand, likely to be stable, or are associated with higher wages. For each, we explain how the occupations are identified and how the information is used. At the end of the chapter, we identify some gaps in existing sources and explain how we will address those gaps with our preferred methodology, with further detail in Chapter Three.

What is the difference between a job and an occupation? In technical terms, a *job* is a singular match between an employee and an employer, while an *occupation* describes the set of jobs that perform similar tasks and roles across many employee-employer matches. But in common parlance, *jobs*, plural, is used in place of *occupation*. We defer to the nomenclature used by the sources in this chapter, but in subsequent chapters we refer to *goal occupations*.

Employment Projections from the Bureau of Labor Statistics

The EP program at the BLS publishes a ten-year projection of job growth in each occupation and industry in the United States. The calculation of the EP is fully transparent: The BLS publishes a handbook detailing each data source used in modeling, the components of the model, how they are calculated, and the assumptions used.

At its simplest, the EP projects how much the economy will grow in the next ten years, what additional goods and services will be demanded with that growth, who makes those goods and provides those services, and how many jobs are required to make and provide them. For example, if the economy grows at 2 percent for ten years, the model predicts how many additional restaurants that would support and, by extension, how many servers, managers, and food preparation jobs those restaurants would require. The EP does this for each of the more than 800 occupations in the United States, addressing the question, "How would employment in industries and occupations grow if the economy were to operate at its full potential a decade from now?" (Horrigan, 2004).

Among several modeling assumptions, the EP projections do not address volatility, such that the EP cannot take short-term job security into account in its projections. The projections speak to long-term job security: They differentiate between occupations that will be less prevalent in the next ten years (i.e., typists) and occupations that will be more prevalent (i.e., software engineers), but the EP does not show which occupations are more vulnerable to cutbacks and layoffs during recessions.

Presented as a table, the EP lists several characteristics for each occupation: current number of jobs and expected number in ten years, percentage of the occupation that is self-employed, number of job openings expected over the next ten years, median annual wage, typical education needed for entry, whether or not the occupation requires experience in a related occupation, and typical amount of on-the-job training (OJT) received. The EP has a sister publication, the *Occupational Outlook Handbook* (OOH), which used to be printed and mailed to U.S. high schools to help career counselors in advising students but is now published online only (BLS, 2021). It combines the statistics from the EP with more-detailed information about the occupation, related occupations, the concentration of the occupation in different states, and other information. The OOH is one of the most widely used sources of career information available.

The EP (and with it the OOH) presents a wealth of information about each of the more than 800 occupations in the United States. With the publication of the data, the BLS releases a series of tables with tabulated occupations, such as fastest growing, fastest declining, highest paying, and others. The EP is an invaluable data source; however, most of the analysis in the data is dedicated to producing the occupational descriptions and projections, rather than analyzing the occupations. We will rely heavily on the EP data in identifying our goal occupations, although, as will be explained in Chapter Three, our method includes additional analyses of the occupations identified.

Middle-Skills Occupations in the EP

Occupations listed in the EP include typical entry-level education requirements. Hence, the rankings of occupations, such as fastest growing, can be filtered by typical educational requirements. According to the BLS's projections, ten of the top 20 occupations in terms of job growth rate and 14 of the top 20 occupations in terms of absolute number of new jobs added between 2018 and 2028 will require less than a bachelor's degree (i.e., no formal educational credential, high school diploma or equivalent, postsecondary nondegree award, and associate degree). In fact, the top four occupations in terms of growth rate require either a high school diploma or a postsecondary nondegree award.

These top four growth rate occupations, their 2018 median pay, the number of new jobs projected, and their projected growth rate are shown in Table 2.1. In the case of solar photovoltaic installers and wind turbine ser-

TABLE 2.1

BLS Top Occupations, by Rate of Forecasted Growth for Subbaccalaureate Occupations

Job Title	2018 Median Pay ($)	2018 Jobs (in thousands)	Projected Number of New Jobs (in thousands)	Projected Growth Rate (%)
Solar photovoltaic installers	42,680	9.6	6.1	63.3
Wind turbine service technicians	54,370	6.7	3.8	56.9
Home health aides	24,200	832.8	304.8	36.6
Personal care aides	24,020	2,420.3	881.0	36.4

SOURCE: BLS, undated, Table 1.3: Fastest Growing Occupations, 2018 and Projected 2028.

vice technicians, the high growth rate can be attributed in part to the very small number of jobs currently in those occupations. But home health aides and personal care aides are both large in number and expected to grow at a rate higher than 30 percent.

Indeed, if instead of growth rate we examined the absolute number of jobs expected to be added, four occupations are both fastest growing and largest growing. In Table 2.2, we show those four occupations: personal care aides, home health aides, software developers, and medical assistants. Only software developers require a bachelor's degree.

State LMI Sponsored by the Department of Labor

States produce state-specific employment projections, similar to the national employment projections, that result in a state-focused list of top growing occupations. These projections are part of a broader federal-state partnership to help job seekers, employers, policymakers, and planners in local areas. For that reason, we explain here the partnership and LMI use for job seekers.

The federal government recognized the importance of local labor market information for job seekers as early as 1933, when it passed the Wagner-Peyser Act creating an Employment Services division within DoL to develop

TABLE 2.2

BLS Top Occupations in Top 30 of Both Total Jobs Projected to be Added and Rate of Growth

Occupation	Typical Entry-Level Education	Rank	
		Absolute Growth	Percentage Growth
Personal care aides	High school diploma or equivalent	1	4
Home health aides	High school diploma or equivalent	4	3
Software developers, applications	Bachelor's degree	6	15
Medical assistants	Postsecondary nondegree award	10	20

SOURCES: BLS, undated, Table 1.3 and Table 1.4: Occupations with the Most Job Growth, 2018 and Projected 2028.

a national system of employment offices to match job seekers to hirers and to develop labor market statistics (Pub. L. 73-30, 1933). This mandate has evolved over time. As part of WIOA, the DoL Employment and Training Administration currently provides grants to states, called Workforce Information Grants to States (WIGS), to finance the production and dissemination of state-specific workforce and labor market information (LMI and occasionally WLMI) (DoL Employment and Training Administration, 1997). The methodology used to produce state LMI is based on the approach used to produce national employment projections. LMI relies on multiple sources of technical support and cross-state coordination to ensure accurate and methodologically consistent information; these sources include the BLS/LMI Oversight Council, the Workforce Information Advisory Council, and the Projections Management Partnership. Additional technical support and training are provided by two state membership programs, the National Association of State Workforce Agencies and the LMI Institute.

So critical is access to reliable information about the labor market that the federal and state governments go to great lengths to produce consistent and timely LMI. LMI is meant to translate the national trends and forces in the economy into near-term effects for states and localities. For example, manufacturing jobs are on the decline in the United States as a result of increased foreign competition and automation. In the national EP, many manufacturing occupations are projected to be less prevalent in the next ten years. But manufacturing workers and manufacturing firms are not evenly spread across the United States, so, while the decline in paper manufacturing has larger consequences for Wisconsin, the decline in auto manufacturing has larger consequences for Michigan. State LMI puts numbers to the state-specific consequences.

State LMI has required products. As part of their WIGS grant, states must produce a Workforce Information Database, state and substate industry and occupation projections, and a statewide economic analysis report.[1] However, states may use this information to create an array of derivative and related products intended for consumption by many users that all fall under the umbrella of state LMI. In Table 2.3, we summarize the three types

TABLE 2.3

Products Derived from State LMI and Their Intended Users

Product Type	Examples	Audience or Intention
Career products	Career Guide Occupation outlooks Occupation training requirements Target/in-demand occupations Transferrable skills/competency models	These products are intended to help job seekers find occupations or make education and training investments.
Economy products	Community/regional economic profiles Economic analysis Economic impact analysis Industry analysis	These products are intended to help policymakers and business leaders understand the economic setting of the state or local area.
Labor market products	Job vacancy surveys Commuting studies Wage and benefit studies Potential applicant pool analysis Labor demographics analysis	These products are intended to help policymakers, business leaders, and educational institutions understand the composition and needs of a state or local area workforce.

SOURCE: Adapted from Poole et al., 2012.

---

[1] WIGS must also be used to train employees on the production and use of WLMI and to produce an annual performance report on all WIGS-financed activities.

of LMI products that states can produce and provide examples of those products and key audiences for the information.

State LMI has a captive audience. For workers, state LMI is intended to help individuals make career decisions and is incorporated into high school and college career counseling, unemployment services counseling, and career counseling at the 2,400 American Job Centers across the United States. For businesses, education institutions, and state and local governments, state LMI is a key tool in planning. An unemployed worker may use LMI, potentially in collaboration with a counselor at an American Job Center, to decide what jobs to apply for, for example, while a community college may use LMI to decide what training courses to offer.

But LMI has shortcomings. Primarily, while states are required to produce certain analyses, many of the derivative products are optional, and their production and dissemination depend on the state. Similarly, while LMI is mandated to be used in certain instances, such as at American Job Centers, some states go above and beyond these requirements to incorporate the insights from LMI in other settings. These state differences mean that LMI has varying utility across states. As an example, in researching this report, we systematically reviewed workforce agencies' websites for the LMI materials disseminated by all 50 states. In general, we looked for state lists identifying high-growth occupations and any accompanying information. Four state websites were either not functioning or did not provide any information. For those that were working, the materials typically included a list of the top in-demand occupations, according to state employment projections. In some states, the LMI materials also included information such as the entry-level educational attainment needed, average wage, and expected annual number of job openings in the state for the occupations in that list.

States can also choose which, if any, occupational groups to highlight beyond a top list of fastest-growing or highest-paying occupations. For example, the Maryland Department of Labor produced a document highlighting cybersecurity occupations. The document outlined the cybersecurity workforce demand by county, the highest-paying occupations within cybersecurity, and the projected employment growth through 2024 (Maryland Department of Labor, 2017). North Dakota produced a document describing high-growth oilfield occupations. Tennessee has a document for construction occupations (Labor Market Information Unit, Tennessee Department of Labor and Workforce Development, undated). Further, states can choose whether to target any groups within job seekers, such as the formerly incarcerated, for example. But outside of listing the occupations projected to have the most growth in that state, states vary in the amount or utility of additional information offered. And they vary in how long the information is posted. While we were researching this report, the North Dakota document was taken down.

However, we should note that in other contexts, such as counseling sessions at American Job Centers or as part of services for unemployed workers, individuals likely delve much more into LMI than is described in public sources.

Middle-Skills Occupations in LMI

Given that the LMI is derived from the EP, LMI has the same classification of typical education required for each occupation. Hence, the ranks of occupations, such as fastest growing, can be filtered by education. Not all states choose to do this when they publicize LMI, but individual LMI sessions will take the person's experience and education into account. In this report, we do not list the LMI recommendations by state for brevity's sake, though we do discuss regional variations in jobs.

Private Sources of Job Prospects

Several private companies also produce lists of "top jobs," "hot jobs," "jobs to watch," and other similar lists. We looked for those products that were most similar to the methodology or interim aim of this report—to find good occupations for workers without a college degree. *U.S. News and World Report* produces numerous lists of best occupations—in addition to best overall, they have separate lists for 12 major industries (e.g., "Best Health Care Jobs," U.S. News and World Report, 2021a) and the highest-paying. Separately, they produce two lists that are intended for workers who did not go to or complete college: "Best Jobs Without a College Degree" and "Highest Paying Jobs Without a Degree" (U.S. News and World Report 2021b, 2021c). To decide which job is best, the staff of *U.S. News and World Report* relies on a composite score of their own design. This score is based on the following factors:

- median salary in the occupation, according to the BLS
- unemployment rate in the occupation, according to the BLS
- job growth, in numbers and percentages, from the BLS EP
- future job prospects, according to the BLS
- stress level, based on interviews and research conducted by the publication's staff and editors
- work-life balance, based on interviews and research conducted by the publication's staff and editors.

This composite score is then summed to produce the "Best Job" ranking. For the ranking of "Highest Paying Jobs," the top "Best Jobs" are re-ranked according to their median salary.

U.S. News and World Report job rankings are fairly comprehensive in their method of scoring, taking into account numerous aspects of a job beyond growth, such as unemployment, pay, and quality of the working conditions. These job lists are also updated annually.[2]

There are a handful of other private sources of job prospects. These are not produced on a regular or repeated basis like *U.S. News and World Report*. They tend to fall into two types. Some are in the vein of quickly assembled lists. One example is from Kiplinger, a media company that specializes in business forecast and personal finance. Job forecasts and prospects are not a regular part of its repertoire; however, it published an article identifying "Best Jobs for the Future" and, similarly, the "Worst Jobs for the Future" (Rapacon, 2018). These lists rely on the BLS Employment Projections and private labor market data from Emsi, an economic modeling company that amalgamates private and public data on the labor market, jobs, workers, and compensation. Kiplinger used these data sources to identify the best and worst occupations, incorporating both projected openings and current median salary in the scores.

---

[2] The *U.S. News* list of the highest-paying and best occupations for workers without a college degree overlapped with the lists that we produced; where it did not, we added their occupations into ours, as we detail in the next chapter.

The other type of job-prospect source consists of more in-depth, one-off research reports to understand broader trends in the economy and their effects on jobs in the future. For example, McKinsey, a private management consulting company, has an economics research division, the McKinsey Global Institute, which produced an in-depth report on *The Future of Work in America* (Lund et al., 2019). The researchers sought to understand the impacts of automation on various occupations. Given that the extent of automation is uncertain, they created multiple automation scenarios and built an economic model, very similar to that used in the BLS employment projections, to estimate the impact of differing levels of automation on each occupation. Pearson, the education company, produced a similarly in-depth report on *The Future of Skills* (Bakhshi et al., 2017). Rather than use EP data, this report used historical employment trends in the Current Population Survey (CPS) between 1983 and 2015 and extrapolated an employment trend to predict whether an occupation would have more demand. Much like our report, the authors then looked at the occupations predicted to be in demand and analyzed the skills in those occupations using data from the Occupational Information Network (O*NET).[3] While these reports provide insight, they are not necessarily useful to practitioners or job seekers.

Middle-Skills Occupations in the Private-Sector Sources

As we noted, *U.S. News and World Report* produces a list of best occupations for workers without a bachelor's degree, which we show in Table 2.4, and highest-paying occupations without a bachelor's degree, which we show in Table 2.5. It is fairly consistent with BLS's projections, which is not surprising, given that *U.S. News and World Report* relies on EP projections for several component inputs. Occupations such as personal care aide, home health aide, wind turbine technician, and physical therapist aide/assistants are among the "best jobs" for individuals without a degree. Furthermore, there is significant overlap between the "best jobs" and the "highest-paying" occupations without a degree, with occupations such as wind turbine tech-

---

[3] We describe the CPS and O*NET in Chapter Three.

TABLE 2.4

U.S. News and World Report's "Best Jobs Without a Degree," 2018

Job Title	Projected New Jobs	Median Salary ($)	Education Needed
Home health aide	304,800	24,200	High school
Medical assistant	154,900	33,610	Postsecondary nondegree
Medical records technician	23,100	40,350	Postsecondary nondegree
Landscaper and groundskeeper	106,400	29,000	Not required
Personal care aide	881,000	24,020	High school
Massage therapist	35,400	41,420	Postsecondary nondegree
Dental assistant	38,700	38,660	Postsecondary nondegree
Solar photovoltaic installer	6,100	42,680	High school
Physical therapist aide	11,300	26,240	High school
Nail technician	15,700	24,330	Postsecondary nondegree
Plumber	68,200	53,910	High school
Insurance sales agent	48,300	50,600	High school
Phlebotomist	29,500	34,480	Postsecondary nondegree
Ophthalmic medical technician	8,900	36,530	Postsecondary nondegree
Licensed practical and licensed vocational nurse	78,100	46,240	Postsecondary nondegree
Electrician	74,100	55,190	High school
Wind turbine technician	3,800	54,370	Postsecondary nondegree
Residential advisor	13,900	27,860	High school
Optician	5,400	37,010	High school

Table 2.4—Continued

Job Title	Projected New Jobs	Median Salary ($)	Education Needed
Esthetician and skincare specialist	7,800	31,290	Postsecondary nondegree
Restaurant cook	299,000	26,530	Not required
Recreation and fitness worker	79,500	29,420	High school
Hairdresser	57,800	24,730	Postsecondary nondegree
Firefighter	17,600	49,620	Postsecondary nondegree
Maintenance and repair worker	85,400	38,300	High school

SOURCE: "Best Jobs Without a Degree," 2018.
NOTE: Order is based on rank according to *U.S. News and World Report*'s scoring criteria.

TABLE 2.5
U.S. News and World Report's "Highest Paying Jobs Without a Degree," 2018

Job Title	Projected New Jobs (Loss)	Median Salary ($)	Education Needed
Patrol officer	34,500	61,380	High school
Executive assistant	(123,000)	59,340	High school
Sales representative	23,300	58,510	High school
Electrician	74,100	55,190	High school
Wind turbine technician	3,800	54,370	Postsecondary nondegree
Structural iron and steelworker	9,200	53,970	High school
Plumber	68,200	53,910	High school
Hearing aid specialist	1,200	52,770	High school
Sound engineering technician	200	52,390	Postsecondary nondegree
Brickmason and blockmason	8,400	50,950	High school
Insurance sales agent	48,300	50,600	High school

Table 2.5—Continued

Job Title	Projected New Jobs (Loss)	Median Salary ($)	Education Needed
Firefighter	17,600	49,620	Postsecondary nondegree
Real estate agent	25,600	48,690	High school
Sheet metal worker	11,400	48,460	High school
Equipment operator	38,500	47,810	High school
Choreographer	(200)	47,800	High school
Surgical technologist	9,700	47,300	Postsecondary nondegree
Carpenter	80,100	46,590	High school
Licensed practical and licensed vocational nurse	78,100	46,240	Postsecondary nondegree
Glazier	5,700	43,550	High school
Cement mason and concrete finisher	21,100	43,000	Not required
Solar photovoltaic installer	6,100	42,680	High school
Bus driver	3,100	41,910	Not required
Insulation contractor	3,100	41,910	Not required
Massage therapist	35,400	41,420	Postsecondary nondegree

SOURCE: "Highest Paying Jobs Without a Degree," 2018.
NOTE: The data are based on the BLS 2018–2028 employment projections (U.S. Bureau of Labor Statistics, undated). Order is based on rank according to *U.S. News and World Report*'s scoring criteria.

nician, patrol officer, solar photovoltaic installer, real estate agent, and surgical technologist making both lists.

Kiplinger's "Best Jobs of the Future" includes six occupations that require less than a bachelor's degree (Rapacon, 2018), which we show in Table 2.6.

The goal of the report from the McKinsey Global Institute was to identify how many jobs would exist in each occupation under different scenarios of automation, so it does not necessarily lend itself perfectly to a comparison of best occupations for workers without a college degree. That said, the report projects that demand for health professionals, STEM professionals,

TABLE 2.6

"Best Jobs of the Future" That Require Less Than a Bachelor's Degree (Kiplinger)

Job Title	Ranking	Total Number of Jobs	Projected Job Growth (2017–2027)	Median Annual Salary ($)	Typical Education
Dental hygienist	11	215,720	20.9%	74,432	Associate
Medical sonographer	16	70,351	23.2%	71,598	Associate
Physical therapist assistant	17	91,319	31.3%	57,429	Associate
Respiratory therapist	18	29,745	22.4%	59,717	Associate
Services sales rep	19	1,100,000	12.5%	51,437	High school diploma
Electrical power-line installer and repairer	26	117,960	16.7%	69,040	High school diploma

SOURCE: Rapacon, 2018.

and health aides and technicians will increase by 48, 37, and 30 percent, respectively, between 2017 and 2030 under a midlevel automation scenario. Further, McKinsey projects that the fastest-growing occupations are massage therapists (88 percent growth in the number of jobs), software developers (79 percent growth), solar photovoltaic installers (70 percent growth), physical therapist aides (69 percent growth), and exercise physiologists (67 percent growth) (Lund et al., 2019). McKinsey's researchers do not sort occupations by education but by a job class of their own design. We show their findings in Table 2.7.

Two Omissions from Existing Public and Private Labor Market Information

As the discussion in this chapter shows, the three major existing sources of labor market information about "good jobs" and "best jobs" can support

TABLE 2.7

McKinsey Projections of Occupational Growth, 2017–2030

Occupation Title	Job Class	Percentage Growth, 2017–2030
Massage therapists	Wealth workers	88
Software developers	Frontier Tech	79
Solar photovoltaic installers	Frontier Tech	70
Physical therapist aides	Healthcare	69
Exercise physiologists	Wealth workers	67
Nurse practitioners	Healthcare	65
Physician assistants	Healthcare	63
Physicians and surgeons	Healthcare	62
Wind turbine service technicians	Frontier Tech	54
Dancers	Creatives	54
Hearing aid specialists	Healthcare	53
Agents of artists and athletes	Wealth workers	49
Dietitians and nutritionists	Wealth workers	48
Nuclear engineers	Frontier Tech	47
Aerospace engineers	Frontier Tech	43
Social and community service managers	Socioemotional support	43
Interior designers	Creatives	42
Multimedia artists and animators	Creatives	41
Occupational therapy aides	Socioemotional support	41
Training and development specialists	Socioemotional support	40
Personal care aides	Healthcare	39
Merchandise displayers and window trimmers	Creatives	37

Table 2.7—Continued

Occupation Title	Job Class	Percentage Growth, 2017–2030
Landscape architects	Wealth workers	34
Musicians and singers	Creatives	34
Electrical engineering technicians	Frontier Tech	33
Actors	Creatives	33
Curators	Creatives	30
Animal caretakers	Wealth workers	29
Clinical, counseling, and school psychologists	Socioemotional support	27
Residential advisers	Socioemotional support	26
Psychologists	Socioemotional support	21

SOURCE: Reproduction of Exhibit 14 from Lund et al., 2019.

career decisionmaking in certain respects. However, two important topics, both relevant to our study given the diversity and youth of ChalleNGe cadets, are not covered in these sources: race and gender disparity in pay; and training, mobility, and career pathways.

Race and Gender Disparity in Pay

While many reviews of good occupations include earnings in some respect, this is often presented as a single aggregated indicator, such as median earnings in the occupation, as seen in *U.S. News and World Report*. But this overlooks an unfortunate aspect of the labor market: entrenched wage inequality between the genders and the races (Daly, Hobijn, and Pedtke, 2017; Graf, Brown, and Patten, 2018; Gould, 2019; Hegewisch and Barsi, 2020). Black workers of either gender earn less than white workers and have higher unemployment, while women of each race earn less than men. Although some of this inequality between groups can be attributed to general wage inequality between workers in the United States, wage gaps also vary by occupation (Blau and Kahn, 2000).

For job seekers, then, knowing that an occupation has a high median salary does not mean that that occupation can ensure them that same median salary. For example, the median earnings of a female accountant are 80 percent of the median earnings of a male accountant; on top of this, black women in financial occupations make less than white women in financial occupations (Hegewisch and Barsi, 2020). *Good* on average does not mean that a job is good for everybody, but most good-occupations lists and publications do not incorporate information concerning disparate opportunity and return.

Training, Mobility, and Career Pathways

A challenge in understanding job quality is to capture a job's relative position, retrospectively, concerning what training or prior jobs were required, and, prospectively, concerning what future jobs may be opened up by experience in a prior job. The minimal educational requirements for a job are much easier to discern, but experience and training are not. A job being classified as *good* does not necessarily mean that it is attainable, that the training or experience requirements are clear or readily known, or that the training is accessible or affordable. Similarly, it is hard to capture the extent to which a job increases future mobility or whether it is a "dead-end" job, and whether a job with physical safety requirements can be a lifelong career.

Take two examples, nail technicians and home health aides. Both are listed in the top ten of *U.S. News and World Report*'s "Best Jobs Without a College Degree" (2018), and both pay a median salary of around $24,000. Nail technicians require a "postsecondary nondegree," according to the rankings. Nail technician programs range in price from $3,000 to $9,000 (Beauty Schools Directory, undated; College Tuition Compare, undated). Home health aides have specific training and certification programs, but certification is required in only about 20 percent of states. Home health aides can work without training or can receive similar credentials, such as the certified nurse's assistant. In practice, both positions are associated with periods of supervised work and logged training hours before working full time. Unfortunately, these occupations are not known to be springboards to future positions (Stone and Bryant, 2019). Both have long hours and, in the case of home health aides, often irregular hours. Moving upward would require additional education or training. The relative position of these two occupations—in that they may require training to enter but also additional training to get to a better job—is hard to convey through a simple ranking.

The same is true for occupations that are associated with high mobility—those that are on a track, which might be called a *career pathway, career ladder,* or *career lattice. Career pathway,* a term common to the education and training world, typically refers to a coordinated education and training investment that builds on itself and leads to good jobs. The College and Career Transitions Initiative defines a career pathway as "a coherent, articulated sequence of rigorous academic and career courses, commencing in ninth grade and leading to an associate degree, an industry-recognized certificate or licensure, or a baccalaureate degree and beyond" (Hughes and Karp, 2006). The Ohio Department of Education defines a career pathway as "a collective look at education and training, wage and outlook information for related occupations. These pathways offer an overview of the various career options along with education and training that can begin as early as grade 7" (Ohio Department of Education, undated).

However, there is growing use of the terms *career ladder* and *career lattice,* which focus on sequences of jobs within an industry, rather than sequences of educational classes. According to Career One Stop from DoL, "career ladders and lattices consist of a group of related jobs that make up a career." They further note that "career ladders display only vertical movement between jobs. In contrast, career lattices contain both vertical and lateral movement, and may reflect more closely the career paths of today's work environment" ("Develop a Career Ladder/Lattice," undated).

In theory, any one occupation, such as medical technician, would be understood as a part of a lattice within health care. Unfortunately, no organization to date has systematically and explicitly identified career pathways within every industry, nor have industry associations or groups all taken to defining or creating lattices. Hence, this type of mobility between jobs, or strength of a job based on the pathway, ladder, or lattice in which it sits, cannot be readily incorporated into good-job lists or rankings. However, this is a growing area of high interest, and at the writing of this report, many states and industries were considering developing career lattice models.

Moreover, unlike career mentoring programs, ChalleNGe's residential setup ends involvement with cadets one year after residency is completed.

Helping a cadet navigate subsequent career mobility is beyond ChalleNGe's capability. Thus, we elect not to consider "gateway" occupations that lead to later "good" occupations as part of a career lattice as a recommendation for ChalleNGe's focus.

How This Report Addresses Gaps in Existing Sources of Labor Market Information

Our methodology seeks to address these two omissions in existing labor market information. Our criteria for identifying "good" middle-skills occupations builds on the standard approach used in previous sources of labor market information on finding *good jobs*—which typically combines expected growth, which implies higher likelihood of being hired, and typical pay—by addressing the two dimensions discussed in the previous section.

First, rather than looking at an occupation's typical or average pay, across all workers, we examine pay within race-by-gender groups. Our method does not exclude all occupations with wage inequality, but we make it a requirement that a *good* occupation is one that is associated with good pay *for all race and gender groups.*

Second, we add a measure of on-the-job growth. Careers can span multiple occupations, especially at the start, but not all jobs invest in workers through training or skill investments. Our method ranks occupations higher when they are associated with these types of investments, recognizing that two occupations—growing at the same rate and paying a similar wage—can have far different career potential based on whether *the worker learns a marketable skill.*

In the next chapter, we walk through our methodology, including the data used, our approach for sorting between degree and nondegree jobs, and the application of our criteria for identifying good middle-skills occupations.

CHAPTER THREE

What Is a Good Job? Part 2—How Good Jobs Are Identified in Our Analyses

In this chapter, we describe the methods and data used in our research. As noted in Chapter One, we take a top-down, occupation-based approach to identifying training investments for ChalleNGe sites. This approach ultimately allows us to identify portable skill sets—rather than specific occupations—that can help cadets succeed across occupations and geographies and, thus, represent a good cross-site investment for ChalleNGe.

The chapter is organized around the research steps presented in Chapter One:

- Define the good occupations, which we call the *goal occupations.*
- Apply empirical definitions to identify the goal occupations, making additional adjustments by occupation family, other rankings, and geographic availability.
- Enumerate and rank the importance of various skills of the goal occupations.
- Narrow the full set of skills to those most commonly ranked as important among the goal occupations.
- Summarize those common skills from an education and training perspective.

Step 1: Define the Criteria for Goal Occupations

In our analysis, we differentiate between an *occupation,* which describes a common set of actions or tasks (i.e., a profession), and *job,* which describes a specific employer-employee match. For example, a lawyer is an example of an occupation, but among lawyers there are good jobs, say at a firm with high pay and upward mobility, and bad jobs, at a firm with low pay and little career advancement. Although *job* and *occupation* are often used interchangeably, this difference is important for our report because we are discussing the skills in an occupation, no matter what the actual job is.

We define *goal occupations* as meeting three qualifications: attainable, high-paying, and growth-oriented. With *attainable,* we are thinking specifically of ChalleNGe cadets and limit the goal occupations to those that do not require a college degree. Cadets can and have gone on to college, but it is not a reasonable, or even informative, prescription to advise site directors that cadets need to go to college to get into good jobs. In addition, a job is not attainable if it is rare or disappearing. Hence, we also define an *attainable* occupation as one that is growing in employment, rather than falling, and has grown in the recent past. With *high-paying,* we are looking for occupations in the upper half of the wage distributions shown in Figure 1.1: an above-median wage for subbaccalaureate workers, both overall and for each race/ethnicity by gender grouping. Finally, with *growth-oriented,* we are looking for occupations whose jobs are often associated with OJT (as reported in O*NET), indicating skill investment by employers. This is partly a reflection of the predictions that middle skills will be in demand and partly a reflection of quality, given that an occupation in which employers routinely invest in employees' skill signals higher quality. Figure 3.1 shows our notional definition of *goal occupations* for cadets.

Step 2: Identify Goal Occupations

Given our definition of attainable, high-paying, growth-oriented occupations, we use publicly available data to identify those occupations using information on the educational distribution of workers in that occupation, the wages of workers in that occupation, past employment growth, projected

FIGURE 3.1

Criteria for Identifying Goal Occupations for Cadets

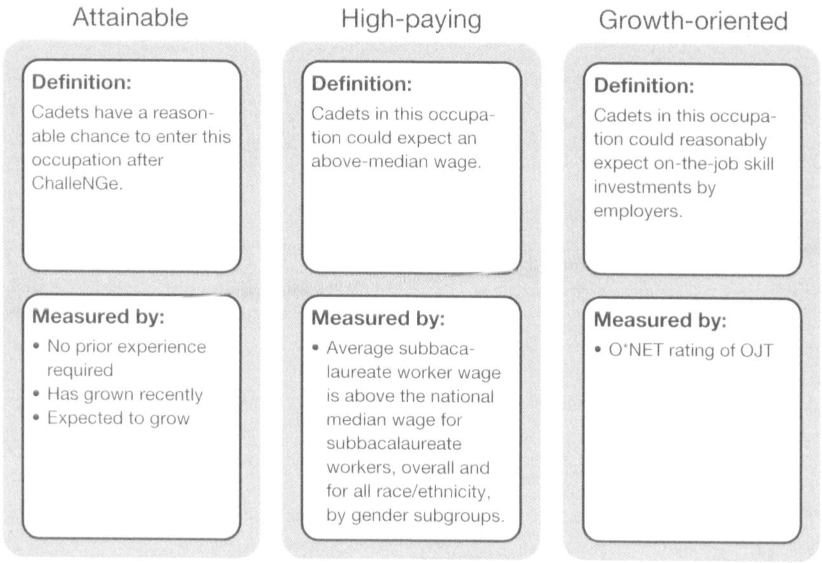

Attainable	High-paying	Growth-oriented
Definition: Cadets have a reasonable chance to enter this occupation after ChalleNGe.	**Definition:** Cadets in this occupation could expect an above-median wage.	**Definition:** Cadets in this occupation could reasonably expect on-the-job skill investments by employers.
Measured by: • No prior experience required • Has grown recently • Expected to grow	**Measured by:** • Average subbaccalaureate worker wage is above the national median wage for subbacalaureate workers, overall and for all race/ethnicity, by gender subgroups.	**Measured by:** • O*NET rating of OJT

employment growth, and ratings of OJT. Unlike previous broad-based lists of "good jobs," as described in Chapter Two, our analysis is focused *only* on occupations that do not require a bachelor's degree.

Data Sets

Our primary data sets are CPS (accessed via the Integrated Public Use Microdata Series, and the EP, both produced by the BLS.[1]

Current Population Survey

The CPS is a nationally representative, monthly survey of about 60,000 households. The CPS collects person-level data on various employment-related characteristics for each member of the household age 15 or older, including labor force participation status (e.g., in the labor force or not in the labor force), employment status (e.g., employed or unemployed), and work

---

[1] Data from the CPS comes from a combination of the Annual Social and Economic Supplement and the Outgoing Rotation Groups.

status (e.g., full-time, part-time for economic reasons but usually full-time, part-time for noneconomic reasons). For purposes of our analysis, we focus on full-time employed persons (i.e., wage/salary employees in the private sector or in government), excluding those who are self-employed. We focus on this population to have a consistent and comparable measure of wage in an occupation. In addition to employment characteristics, the CPS contains detailed data on industry, occupational titles, wages, hours usually worked, and demographic data (e.g., race, ethnicity, gender, educational attainment).

Employment Projections

We discussed the EP at length in Chapter Two. The EP program at the BLS publishes a ten-year projection of job growth in each occupation and industry in the United States.

Of importance to our study, the unit of observation in the EP and CPS differ. In the EP, the unit of observation is the occupation—the current and projected employment, the median earnings, and other occupation features. In the CPS, the unit of observation is the worker—their age, gender, race, wages, and their occupation. We use both the official statistics about the occupation in the EP and the information about workers in an occupation from the CPS in evaluating our criteria.

This is not without challenges. The EP (using the Standard Occupational Classification, or SOC, codes) and the CPS (using CPS codes) employ different classification schemes for coding and describing occupations, with the EP providing a finer level of detail. There is a crosswalk between the two numeric classification systems, the National Employment Matrix/SOC to CPS Crosswalk. This crosswalks SOC occupation codes used by the employment projections to the distinct occupation codes used by the CPS.

However, at times, more than one occupation in the EP matches to a single occupation in the CPS, and vice versa. This can become an issue, say, if the two occupations in the CPS have very different demographics but are listed as a single occupation in the EP. We discuss this issue in more detail in the next section.

Identifying Subbaccalaureate Occupations

We start by narrowing the more than 800 total U.S. occupations in our data sources to only those that do not necessitate a four-year college degree. We refer to these as *subbaccalaureate occupations*. We define a *subbaccalaureate occupation* as one in which fewer than 35 percent of job holders have at least a bachelor's degree in the CPS (implying that approximately two-thirds of workers in the occupation do not have a bachelor's degree).

This was not a straightforward estimation. In theory, all jobs within an occupation have a discrete educational requirement, and all workers in that occupation would have exactly that level of education (this assumes workers do not pursue further education out of general interest). However, in practice, this type of uniformity is not often the case, especially if the occupation or the worker has lower educational attainment. All jobs within the occupation of medical doctor, for example, require an MD (or similar advanced degree), and all doctors have such degrees. At the same time, education levels among home health aides vary: A postsecondary certificate is required in certain localities and situations but not in others, and in many instances, workers have more than a postsecondary certificate. Workers can and do work in occupations in which they have more education than they need. However, if a significant portion of the workers in an occupation have a bachelor's degree, a prospective worker without one could have a difficult time finding employment. Bachelor's degrees have documented signaling value, and a worker without one will be at a comparative disadvantage (Heywood and Wei, 2004).

For each occupation, we looked at the share of workers who did not have a bachelor's degree. We found in comparing the distribution of these shares that there was an inflection around 65 percent, and we chose that as our cutoff. Any occupation with more than 35 percent of workers with a bachelor's degree (less than 65 percent subbaccalaureate) was cut.[2]

We identified this set of occupations in the CPS and then merged them to the EP to compare the observed education distribution in the CPS with the stated entry education noted in the EP. However, the number of CPS

---

[2] The inflection is the change in slopes of the distribution of occupations by shares of workers with a college degree before and after 65 percent. The slope before was flatter and after was steeper.

occupations is smaller than the number of EP occupations, so that there are sometimes multiple EP occupations for a single CPS occupation, and frequently those multiple EP occupations have different entry education levels listed. For example, in the EP, the entry-level education requirement for a web developer is an associate degree, while the entry-level education requirement for a systems analyst is a bachelor's degree. However, both these occupations fall under the same occupation code in the CPS (computer scientists and systems analysts/network systems analysts/web developers).[3]

We heuristically developed four education categories to indicate that the education level is not uniform within an occupation:

- **Definitely no postsecondary:** All EP occupations that map to the CPS occupation require either no formal education or a high school diploma or equivalent.
- **Mixed postsecondary:** EP occupations that map to the CPS occupation require a mix of high school diploma or equivalent (including no formal education), postsecondary nondegree award (such as a certificate), some college but no degree, or an associate degree.
- **Definitely postsecondary:** All EP occupations that map to the CPS occupation require a mix of postsecondary nondegree award or an associate degree.
- **Mixed baccalaureate:** The EP occupations that map to the CPS occupation require a mix of postsecondary nondegree award, some college but no degree, associate degree, and bachelor's degree.

We use these categories in describing the goal occupations once we have identified them.

Applying the Criteria for Identifying Good Occupations

As noted in Step 1 above, we have three criteria for identifying good occupations among those that are subbaccalaureate: attainable, high-paying, and growth-oriented. Our criteria are a direct reflection of the population for

---

[3]   Only 25 percent of workers in this collective occupation lack a bachelor's degree, so this occupation is classified as requiring a bachelor's degree.

whom we are preparing this report: the cadets in the Youth ChalleNGe program. These are young workers who are geographically distributed across the country, who likely have very little work experience, and who are looking for good jobs or, short of that, jobs that will help them later advance into good jobs. We developed multiple ways to measure each criterion.

Attainable

A good occupation must be **attainable**. To measure attainability, we use the EP projections of whether the number of jobs in an occupation is expected to grow over the next ten years. This is a common "good jobs" metric—in some cases, the only metric. We also look at whether the number of jobs in the occupation grew over the last business cycle in the CPS.[4] An *attainable* job is one that has grown and is expected to grow in the future (yes/no classification, not a level-based measure). The EP also contains assessments of whether work experience in a related occupation is a prerequisite for employment. We incorporate this variable as a measure of attainability: Occupations requiring any prior experience are considered not attainable.

High-Paying

A good occupation must also be **high-paying**. There are many ways to measure how well a job pays. Most "good jobs" lists include, or rank by, median wage. While that might work for an ordinal list, it does not create any natural exclusion or help narrow down the total number of occupations into a subset. For that reason, we use the hourly wages observed in the CPS to define *high-paying*: An occupation is high-paying if the subbaccalaureate workers in that occupation earned a higher wage than the median wage of subbaccalaureate workers across all occupations in at least two of the four years of the period we analyzed (2015–2018). As shown in Figure 3.2, the majority of occupations meet this requirement in zero or all years, meaning we would not get very different results by making the cutoff a different number of years.

---

[4] For past growth we look at business cycle, which started at the trough of the 2007 recession (in 2009). We look at growth during a period of economic growth to give occupations the best chance for growth, rather than judging them over a period that includes economic contraction (i.e., starting our analysis in 2008).

FIGURE 3.2

The Share of Occupations with Wages Above the Median over a Four-Year (2015–2018) Period

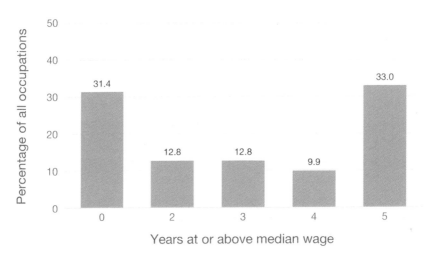

SOURCE: U.S. Census Bureau, BLS, undated.

However, as we noted in Chapter Two, wage inequality is a serious concern in the labor market. The difference in pay between genders and races—the pay gap—is estimated by economists through regression analysis, which controls for other features of the worker, such as age and education. We did not want to calculate the pay gap for every occupation in the subbaccalaureate group—first, because there were concerns about having sufficient sample size, and second, because the results would be less instructive. An occupation with a smaller pay gap may be indicative of a more inclusive culture, but an occupation with a small pay gap where everyone earns less than a family-sustaining wage is still not a good recommendation for a career. Considering this, we opted for the same "top-half" cutoff that we used for the wages of all workers, and applied that to the wages of each of the eight race/ethnicity (black, white, Hispanic, Asian) and gender (male, female) groups. We elected to use the median rather than the mean to avoid distributional distortion from extremely high or low wages. We consider a subbaccalaureate occupation to be *high-paying* for black female workers if the black female workers in an occupation earn a higher wage than the median wage of all black female subbaccalaureate workers. In sum, we rate occupations as *high-paying* if they are high-paying for *every* demographic group that we consider, rather than just for *some* demographic groups.

Growth-Oriented

Finally, occupations must be **growth-oriented**. We measure exclusively using the EP, which includes an assessment of the amount of OJT in an occupation. There are four categories of OJT: none, short-term OJT (one month or less), moderate-term OJT (between one and 12 months), and long-term OJT (more than 12 months). We anticipate that for jobs with more OJT, employers are generally more invested in the long-term careers of their employees, and thus we use this as a proxy for the longer-term career potential of an occupation, whether the potential is in that specific occupation or another occupation. For example, within health occupations, "aide" occupations typically have short-term OJT, several "technician" occupations have moderate-term OJT, and dispensing opticians are the sole subbaccalaureate occupation with long-term OJT. Note that apprenticeships are not classified as OJT.

OJT is not the only measure of employers' investment in workers' skill or careers, but it is one that is systematically measured in a publicly available data set. It is also not the only aspect of a job's potential in terms of career dividends. As we noted in our prior discussion of career pathways, there is growing interest in, but sparse research or metrics yet developed, in thinking of jobs as being one part of a career pathway or career lattice. Future research into evaluating good jobs could take this pathway component, once systematically developed, into account.

Limitations

Note that we do not include any measure of nonwage compensation or benefits, which can greatly affect the day-to-day quality of a job. Having flexible hours, paid vacation, or good health insurance are all important dimensions of a job, but they are beyond the scope of this analysis because they vary too much by state and employer policy rather than occupation or skill group. We are unable to incorporate any systematic data on prestige or job satisfaction. We also do not consider usual hours. Our analysis is based on full-time workers—but those workers' hours could be unrepresentative of the majority of workers in that job who do not work full time. Usual hours could reflect a labor market constraint (there are not more hours available) or a worker preference for less than full-time work. Because we do not have a way of distinguishing between the part-time workers in an occupation who are constrained versus not, we did not consider usual hours.

Scoring the Occupations

We measure each of the criteria—attainable, high-paying, growth-oriented—along the dimensions discussed. Dimensions are either rated "yes/no," or, for OJT, are translated from a score of 0 (no OJT) to 3 (high OJT). Table 3.1 gives the distribution of occupation ratings across each category. There are 332 subbaccalaureate occupations in the final data set.

Assessment

In general, we find that a scant few subbaccalaureate occupations meet every dimension listed in Table 3.1. Instead, their performance in these numeric tests serves as a starting point and base for assessment. Within each occupation family, we examined all of the subbaccalaureate occupations across the metrics we designed and came up with a score based on the number of metrics scored as "yes." Those with at least a 90-percent "yes rate" were included in the goal occupations. Given that OJT is highly variable, we considered OJT a "bonus" for occupations with scores that fell short of the 90-percent threshold. We also considered the variance of the underlying metrics. For example, within the management occupations, purchasing agents and buyers meet most of our criteria, but the occupations have high internal variance on reported education and training (why the "easy to get" field is blank).

Our assessment encompasses several additional dimensions. To start, we also consider the recommendations from other sources. Despite their differing methodologies, there is significant overlap across the public and private sources regarding specific occupations with a promising outlook for individuals without a four-year college degree. We summarize the occupations appearing multiple times in other lists, which we term the *frequent flyers*, in Table 3.2. The majority of the occupations frequently identified by other sources are in the health care sector, but several occupations, such as solar photovoltaic installers, wind turbine technicians, landscapers, and

TABLE 3.1

Summary of Nonbaccalaureate Occupations in Criteria Dimensions

Category	Yes	No
No prior experience required ("easy to get")	273	41
Grew in 2010–2018	162	172
Projected to grow in 2018–2028	221	113
High-paying over all subbaccalaureate workers	145	189
High-paying for Black male	216	103
High-paying for Black female	232	87
High-paying for Hispanic male	193	126
High-paying for Hispanic female	232	87
High-paying for White male	157	162
High-paying for White female	189	130
High-paying for all other male	234	85
High-paying for all other female	257	62
Has low OJT	120	
Has moderate OJT	141	
Has high OJT	35	

SOURCE: Authors' calculations using CPS extracts.
NOTE: There are some cases in which multiple occupations in the EP map to one occupation in the CPS. Hence, there may be occupations rated with both low- and moderate on-the-job training, and we count both of these in the above tabulations.

sales representatives, to name a few, provide opportunities in other fields for individuals without a bachelor's degree. This listing serves as a validation of and comparison with our methodology. We consider each frequent flyer as a potential addition to our goal occupations list, and if it does not meet our criteria, we indicate the rationale in the final column.

In addition, we also assess the occupations in the context of their occupation family; for example, architectural drafters are part of the architec-

TABLE 3.2

Frequent Flyer Occupations Among the "Good Jobs" Lists

Occupation (alternate title from CPS)	Attainable	High-Paying	Growth (OJT)	Goal Occupation
Home health aide	Yes	No	1	No
Dental assistant	Mixed	No	0	No
Insurance sales agent	Yes	No	2	No
Landscape architect, landscaper, and groundskeeper	Yes	No	2	No
Massage therapist	Mixed	No	0	No
Medical assistant, medical secretary	Yes	No	2	No
Nurse assistant, practitioner, and licensed practical/vocational nurse	Yes	Yes	0	Yes
Personal care aide	Yes	No	1	No
Pharmacy technician (Health Diagnosing and Treating Practitioner Support Technician)	Yes	Yes	2	Yes
Phlebotomist (Medical Assistants and Other Healthcare Support, not elsewhere classified)	Yes	No	0	No
Physical therapist assistant and aide	Yes	Yes	1	Yes
Sales representative, service sale representative	Mixed	No	2	No
Software developer	NA	NA	NA	Yes
Solar photovoltaic installer (Construction worker, not elsewhere classified)	Yes	Yes	2	Yes
Wind turbine technician	NA	NA	NA	Yes

SOURCES: Authors' summary of BLS, undated, Table I.3. Fastest growing occupations, 2018 and projected 2028; "Best Jobs Without a Degree," 2018; Rapacon, 2018; and Lund et al., 2019.
NOTE: NA = occupation was not enumerated in the CPS.

ture and engineering family. Although drafters are not expected to grow over the next ten years, the occupation family is expected to grow and is associated with fast wage growth. In addition to the wage and employment growth context, occupation families can help us understand whether the occupation has the potential for a career pathway, even if our ability to infer is limited by the lack of industry-published pathways. We provide a detailed discussion of each occupation family in Appendix A.

Finally, a key aspect of attainability that is not part of the numeric dimensions in Table 3.1 is the geographic availability of jobs within an occupation. Certain extraction jobs, for example, are highly lucrative and expected to grow in the next ten years but are very concentrated in a few locations. As the aim of the report is to identify cross-site skill investments, we exclude occupations that are not broadly geographically available. We provide a discussion of geographic variation in occupations in Appendix B, as well as a geographic summary of the selected goal occupations.

Step 3: Enumerate the Skills of Goal Occupations

Our next step is to enumerate the skills of goal occupations, which we do using the O*NET database. The O*NET is the occupational database of characteristics, work requirements, and work conditions for occupations within the United States economy. It is intended to help individuals research careers that fit with their personality, interests, and preferences, in addition to helping employers find skilled workers. For each occupation in the United States, the O*NET uses surveys of job holders and occupational experts to define the characteristics of the occupation across several subject areas.

The O*NET surveys job holders and occupational experts using the same questionnaires, then summarizes the responses to characterize the occupation. The questionnaires have eight parts, which correspond to the eight categories of occupation characteristics published on O*NET: abilities, interests, work values, generalized work activities, knowledge, skills, work contexts, and work styles. These are referred to as the O*NET *domains*, and the characteristics within the domains are the *elements*. For example, within the domain of ability there is an element called *arm-hand steadiness*, which is the ability to keep your hand and arm steady while moving your arm or while holding your arm and hand in one position. For each element in the domain, respondents answer two questions:

- How important is [the specific ability] to your current job?
- What level of [the specific ability] is needed to perform your current job?

The exception to this is the work context domain, which asks how frequently the element is used on the job.

Although the importance and frequency questions have uniform responses (ranging from "1 not important" to "5 extremely important"), the level of ability is measured on a seven-part scale whose responses are written for the element in question with three anchoring examples. For example, arm-hand steadiness ranges from 1 "light a candle" to 4 "thread a needle" to 7 "cut facets in a diamond." All of which is to say, the O*NET provides an incredible amount of detail about an occupation; each element has two measures, one of level and the other of importance, and there are numerous elements within the eight domains. We map six of the eight O*NET domains—abilities, skills, knowledge, work activities, work contexts, and work styles—to the goal occupations identified in the previous step. More detail on the individual elements of each domain is available in Appendix C.

For our work, we use the importance measure (this harmonizes well with the frequency measure for activities). Since we are focused on entry-level jobs for which workers have little to no prior experience, level of ability is not as useful a dimension as importance (Burrus et al., 2013). In addition, research has indicated that there exists a strong correlation between importance and level ratings (for example, if an attribute is rated as not important, level is generally zero) (Handel, 2016).

O*NET is not a perfect data set. To start, there are several overlapping elements across the domains. There are three measures of mathematics in the occupation: one in skills, one in abilities, and one in knowledge. Similar overlap exists for such topics as decisionmaking, writing, communication, and others. To make sure that clusters of similar elements do not crowd out other elements through this type of repetition, we assess each domain separately and do not compare elements from different domains, ensuring that "mathematics" does not claim three places unless it is the top skill, ability, and knowledge element.

A separate issue is that the O*NET tends to give much more detail about manufacturing than other occupations. By looking only at what is ranked as important in the occupation, we keep superfluous measures of the physical component of jobs from clouding our analysis. But there could be aspects of an occupation not captured as well, or in as much detail, in comparison.

Despite these caveats, the O*NET is an established resource for researchers interested in labor markets, employment outcomes, workforce development, job exposures, and other fields. The O*NET has been used to assess the most important competencies for specific careers and measure the changing workforce demands by education level (Burrus et al., 2013). It has also been used to identity the relationship between occupational characteristics and income (Huang and Pearce, 2013). And, prescient to the current time, researchers have also used specific O*NET categories to assess job exposures, such as occupational exposures workers face during a pandemic (Cifuentes et al., 2010). The O*NET is thus employed as a realistic reflection of job content and characteristics.

Step 4: Find the Common Skills Among Goal Occupations

We next examined six domains in the O*NET and compared the importance of elements within those domains across goal occupations and between goal occupations that are associated with less or more education. Three of these domains directly translate to classroom instruction—knowledge, skills, and abilities. The other three—work activities, work contexts, and work styles—provide context for the work environment and give further insight into the importance of the classroom elements.

We empirically ranked the elements within each domain according to the average importance score across occupations in the analysis group (e.g., goal occupations, subbaccalaureate occupations). We then reproduced the top ten elements and compared these elements in the goal occupations and all subbaccalaureate occupations and also compared goal occupations that require more or less education. By taking the (unweighted) average, we can look for elements that are ranked as important across all or most of the occupations. By looking for the common skills among goal occupations in the O*NET, we are by definition ignoring occupation-specific skills. Instead, those that are shared across occupations are potentially high-return investments for a program such as ChalleNGe.

Step 5: Summarize the Common Skills from an Education Perspective

In our final step, we grouped the elements necessary for the goal occupations into themes to focus the discussion of how to make broad skill investments in the classroom. However, not all skills are readily or easily teachable. Once we identified the common skills from the goal occupations, we determined how well those skills translate into the classroom, identified areas of overlap with skills currently taught in the ChalleNGe program, and made recommendations for how ChalleNGe could incorporate more skills, particularly in the program's residential phase.

In the next chapter, we present our goal occupations. Although the ultimate purpose of our occupation list is to use it as a means of identifying marketable middle skills, we understand that the list itself provides insight into career opportunities, similar to other sources of data on "good jobs" that we presented in Chapter Two.

Our occupation list, and the skills associated with those occupations, is not the only way to arrive at identifying potential occupational investments. Not only are there many measures of good jobs, but there are also ways (outside of the O*NET) to measure skill requirements. Many private job posting sites enumerate openings and skill requirements. A separate approach could have identified in-demand skills by aggregating job postings. There are trade-offs to the approaches. Only a subset of job openings are ever advertised in online postings, making them not representative of all career options. Furthermore, job postings are temporary, and while they do give a summary of skills needed, the set of the current openings can change depending on current economic conditions. By looking over many years of growth and wages, we hope to extend the utility of this report's findings over a longer period.

CHAPTER FOUR

Finding 1—The Goal Occupations ("Good Jobs") for Workers Without a College Degree

In this chapter, we present the set of middle-skills occupations, which we call the goal occupations, that met the majority of our three criteria: They are attainable, high-paying, and growth-oriented. We present a list of the goal occupations and the occupation groups, or families, which they come from. Our list of occupations is about helping cadets build long-term skills, not find near-term jobs. These occupations represent an interim step in the study, but ChalleNGe sites can also use this list as a cross reference to help find locally or regionally based lists of good jobs in their states.

It is important to note that this list of occupations should not be thought of as a set of requirements or even guidance for job placement in the post-residential phase. ChalleNGe youth are 16 to 19 years old when they finish the residential component of the program, and many have limited or no prior work experience. Occupations that we do not highlight, such as food service, offer a chance for new workers to demonstrate basic workplace skills, such as accountability, showing up on time, and following directions. These jobs require little in the way of unique skill training or prior experience. They are also nearly always low-paying. In that sense, they are not informative of high-return skill investments. However, early positive work experience can provide a high return in the context of an individual's career trajectory.

The Goal Occupations

Both the CPS and the EP organize occupations into categories, or families, of similar occupations. Health occupations, for example, include doctors, nurses, technicians, assistants, and home health aides. In total, we identified 102 goal occupations (detailed discussion of selection is found in Appendix A) that fell into two types: those from occupation families that had mixed education backgrounds, such as health, and those from occupation families that were mostly, or entirely, occupations that do not require a college degree, such as service. The former tends to include technician or assistant positions working under highly educated workers, while the latter run the gamut from construction workers to office clerks.

In Table 4.1, we total the number of occupations in a family, the number of occupations that do not require a high school diploma, and the number that we identify as goal occupations for three groups of occupation families: those with mixed educational requirements and those with lower educational requirements that do and do not have goal occupations.

As we noted in Chapter Two, many growth projections predict that high-skilled occupations, particularly in science, technology, engineering, and math, will lead job growth in the coming year. Subbaccalaureate occupations in these areas and work with those high-skilled workers met all our criteria for goal occupations. Even within these mixed-education occupation families, we did not include all subbaccalaureate occupations. In management, for example, even the subbaccalaureate jobs required years of prior experience, such as manager at a construction company. And in health, many

TABLE 4.1

Summary of Occupation Families, Number of Subbaccalaureate Occupations, and Number of Goal Occupations

Occupation Family	Number of Occupations	Number of Subbaccalaureate Occupations	Number of Goal Occupations
Mixed/high-education occupation families			
Management[a]	46	11	2
Computer and mathematical	11	3	2

Table 4.1—Continued

Occupation Family	Number of Occupations	Number of Subbaccalaureate Occupations	Number of Goal Occupations
Engineering and science[b]	36	7	7
Legal and education[c]	20	4	2
Arts and entertainment	16	6	1
Health[d]	35	17	13
Low-education occupation families with goal occupations			
Protective service	13	13	4
Office and administrative support	50	49	16
Construction	29	29	24
Installation, maintenance, and repair	34	34	25
Transportation and material moving	29	29	5
Low-education occupation families without goal occupations			
Food preparation and serving	11	11	0
Building and grounds cleaning and maintenance	6	6	0
Personal care and service	18	18	0
Sales and related	17	17	0
Extraction	5	5	0
Production	71	71	0

SOURCES: Author compilations of BLS data.

[a] *Management* spans CPS categories Management in Business, Science and Arts; Business Operation Specialists; Financial Specialists.

[b] *Engineering and science* spans CPS categories Architecture and Engineering; Technicians; Life, Physical, and Social Sciences.

[c] *Legal and education* spans CPS categories Community and Social Services; Legal; Education, Training, and Library.

[d] *Health* spans CPS categories Healthcare Practitioners and Technicians and Healthcare Support.

subbaccalaureate jobs were low-paying for nearly every worker group, such as home health aide. In arts and entertainment, many occupations required little explicit training or experience but are not widely available or plausible for all individuals (due to the underlying talent requirement).

In the lower-education occupation families, the occupations added to the goal list varied. In construction and installation and maintenance, most of the occupations made it onto the list of goal occupations. In addition to growing in number, these jobs are associated with apprenticeship, job mobility, and OJT. In others, such as office support, where many jobs are becoming obsolete, we only added a select handful; the same is true for transportation and protective service.

Critically, there are six occupation families without any goal occupations: Food Preparation and Service, Buildings and Grounds Cleaning and Maintenance, Personal Care and Service, Sales and Related, Extraction, and Production. The first four are examples of occupations that can be useful in demonstrating employability but are not recommended as long-term careers with appropriate potential for upward mobility. Extraction and production occupations can be highly lucrative but do not have broad availability. Extraction is geographically concentrated in areas with relevant natural resources, such as Texas and North Dakota. Production (manufacturing) is more geographically widespread, but availability and skill needs vary considerably by employer.

The goal occupations themselves are listed in Table 4.2. For each, we give the name of the occupation family, the occupation, and the education level. Recall that, based on education requirements in the EP and observed among workers in jobs, we have four education categories within subbaccalaureate:

- **No postsecondary:** No education beyond a high school diploma is required.
- **Mixed postsecondary:** Workers and jobs within this occupation have a mix of high school degrees, postsecondary nondegree awards (such as occupation credentials or certificates), and associate degrees.
- **Postsecondary:** The occupation requires a postsecondary nondegree award or an associate degree.

- **Mixed baccalaureate:** Workers and jobs in this occupation have a mix of postsecondary nondegree awards, associate degrees, and bachelor's degrees.

Like the occupation families they come from, occupations in the mixed education families tend to require postsecondary awards, such as an associate degree or a nondegree award. However, being listed as "no postsecondary" does not equate to requiring no skills training or post–high school

TABLE 4.2

Goal Occupations and Their Associated Formal Education Level

Family	Occupation	Education Level
Management	Claims adjuster, appraiser, examiner, and investigator	Mixed postsecondary
	Tax preparer	No postsecondary
Computer and mathematical	Web developer	Postsecondary
	Computer support specialist	Mixed postsecondary
Engineering and science	Drafter	Postsecondary
	Engineering technician, except drafter	Postsecondary
	Surveying and mapping technician	No postsecondary
	Agricultural and food science technician	Postsecondary
	Chemical technician	Postsecondary
	Geological and petroleum technician and nuclear technician	Postsecondary
	Life, physical, and social science technician, not elsewhere classified	Mixed baccalaureate
Arts and entertainment	Broadcast and sound engineering technician and radio operator, and media and communication equipment workers, all other	Mixed postsecondary
Legal and education	Paralegal and legal assistant	Postsecondary
	Legal support worker, not elsewhere classified	Mixed postsecondary

Table 4.2—Continued

Family	Occupation	Education Level
Health	Radiation therapist	Postsecondary
	Respiratory therapist	Postsecondary
	Clinical laboratory technologist and technician	Postsecondary
	Dental hygienist	Postsecondary
	Diagnostic related technologist and technician	Postsecondary
	Emergency medical technician and paramedic	Postsecondary
	Health diagnosing and treating practitioner support technician	Mixed postsecondary
	Licensed Practical and Licensed Vocational Nurse	Postsecondary
	Medical records and health information technician	Postsecondary
	Optician, dispensing	No postsecondary
	Health technologist and technician, not elsewhere classified	Mixed baccalaureate
	Occupational therapy assistant and aide	Mixed postsecondary
	Physical therapist assistant and aide	Mixed postsecondary
Protective service	Firefighter	Postsecondary
	Fire inspector	Mixed postsecondary
	Police officer and detective	No postsecondary
	Animal control	No postsecondary
Office and administrative support	Communications equipment operator, all other	No postsecondary
	Billing and posting clerk	No postsecondary
	Gaming cage worker	No postsecondary
	Financial clerk, not elsewhere classified	No postsecondary
	Brokerage clerk	No postsecondary
	Court, municipal, and license clerk	No postsecondary
	Eligibility interviewer, government programs	No postsecondary
	Interviewer, except eligibility and loan	No postsecondary
	Loan interviewer and clerk	No postsecondary

Table 4.2—Continued

Family	Occupation	Education Level
Office and administrative support	Reservation and transportation ticket agent and travel clerk	No postsecondary
	Information and record clerk, all other	No postsecondary
	Cargo and freight agent	No postsecondary
	Courier and messenger	No postsecondary
	Dispatcher	No postsecondary
	Production, planning, and expediting clerk	No postsecondary
	Insurance claims and policy processing clerk	No postsecondary
Construction	Boilermaker	No postsecondary
	Brickmason, blockmason, and stonemason	No postsecondary
	Carpenter	No postsecondary
	Carpet, floor, and tile installers and finisher	No postsecondary
	Cement mason, concrete finisher, and terrazzo worker	No postsecondary
	Paving, surfacing, and tamping equipment operator	No postsecondary
	Construction equipment operator except paving, surfacing, and tamping equipment operator	No postsecondary
	Drywall installer, ceiling tile installer, and taper	No postsecondary
	Electrician	No postsecondary
	Glazier	No postsecondary
	Insulation worker	No postsecondary
	Pipelayer, plumber, pipefitter, and steamfitter	No postsecondary
	Plasterer and stucco mason	No postsecondary
	Reinforcing iron and rebar worker	No postsecondary

Table 4.2—Continued

Family	Occupation	Education Level
Construction	Roofer	No postsecondary
	Sheet metal worker, metal-working	No postsecondary
	Structural iron and steel worker	No postsecondary
	Construction and building inspector	No postsecondary
	Elevator installer and repairer	No postsecondary
	Fence erector	No postsecondary
	Hazardous materials removal worker	No postsecondary
	Highway maintenance worker	No postsecondary
	Rail-track laying and maintenance equipment operator	No postsecondary
	Construction worker, not elsewhere classified	No postsecondary
Installation, maintenance, and repair	Avionics technician	Postsecondary
	Electric motor, power tool, and related repairer	No postsecondary
	Electrical and electronics repairer, transportation equipment, and industrial and utility	Postsecondary
	Security and fire alarm systems installer	No postsecondary
	Aircraft mechanic and service technician	Postsecondary
	Automotive body and related repairer	No postsecondary
	Automotive glass installer and repairer	No postsecondary
	Automotive service technician and mechanic	Postsecondary
	Bus and truck mechanics and diesel engine specialist	No postsecondary
	Heavy vehicle and mobile equipment service technician and mechanic	No postsecondary
	Small engine mechanic	Mixed postsecondary
	Control and valve installer and repairer	No postsecondary
	Heating, air conditioning, and refrigeration mechanic and installer	Postsecondary

Table 4.2—Continued

Family	Occupation	Education Level
Installation, maintenance, and repair	Home appliance repairer	No postsecondary
	Industrial and refractory machinery mechanic	No postsecondary
	Maintenance and repair workers, general	No postsecondary
	Maintenance worker, machinery	No postsecondary
	Millwright	No postsecondary
	Electrical powerline installer and repairer	No postsecondary
	Telecommunications line installer and repairer	No postsecondary
	Precision instrument and equipment repairer	Mixed postsecondary
	Coin, vending, and amusement machine servicer and repairer	No postsecondary
	Rigger	No postsecondary
	Helper—installation, maintenance, and repair worker	No postsecondary
	Other installation, maintenance, and repair worker, including wind turbine service technician, commercial diver, and signal and track switch repairer	Mixed postsecondary
Transportation and material moving	Bus and ambulance driver and attendant	No postsecondary
	Driver/sales worker and truck driver	Mixed postsecondary
	Motor vehicle operator, all other	No postsecondary
	Subway, streetcar, and other rail transportation worker	No postsecondary
	Transportation inspector	No postsecondary

education investments. Many construction occupations, for example, are associated with apprenticeships. A lack of systematic data collection on occupational licenses and certifications (and their variation in use by state and by industry) means that we also do not capture these credentials in our hierarchy of "postsecondary education level." This simple education map is loosely informative of whether the occupation is associated with an up-front education investment.

Note that the list of occupations in Table 4.2 is not meant to be an exhaustive set of career recommendations for cadets who have recently completed ChalleNGe—there may be additional good occupations to recommend based on a given cadet's intended work location. Rather, we selected this set as a relatively universally accessible group of occupations to study the job skills required for these occupations so that the ChalleNGe curriculum can be aligned to promote relevant skill development. These occupations are the basis for the skill and job attribute analysis that follows in Chapter Five.

Finding 2—The Skills and Capabilities Common to the Goal Occupations ("Good Jobs")

In this chapter, we identify skills that are common across many good jobs. Using the list of goal occupations identified in Chapter Four, we examine the skills those occupations require. Rather than focusing on occupation-specific skills, we are looking for common skills shared by many goal occupations. We identify these skills using the O*NET produced by the DoL.

As explained in Chapter Three, the O*NET is a database of descriptors for each occupation in the United States. It has eight categories of descriptions, called domains, and numerous elements within the domains. Each element is measured by its importance to an occupation. For example, one domain is "work activities," and one element within that domain is "interacting with computers," which will have a number 1 to 5 that measures how important or frequent interacting with computers is to the job. To understand how important an element like "interacting with computers" is among the goal occupations, we simply average the measure (1 to 5) that was given for that element among the 102 goal occupations.

For example, one element in the knowledge domain is *customer and personal service*, defined as "Knowledge of principles and processes for providing customer and personal services. This includes customer needs assessment, meeting quality standards for services, and evaluation of customer satisfaction," and one goal occupation is occupational therapy aide (O*NET 31-2011; O*NET Online, 2021d). Among occupational therapy aides, knowledge of customer and personal service measures at 4.1, which is very important. Averaged across all goal occupations, personal care and service is 3.48, between important and very important.

To put that average among goal occupations in context, we make two comparisons:

1. **Goal occupations versus all subbaccalaureate occupations.** We compare the average importance rank of each element among the 102 goal occupations and all 330 subbaccalaureate occupations.

2. **Less-education goal occupations versus more-education goal occupations.** We compare the importance rank of each element, dividing the goal occupations into two groups. *Less education* refers to our previous categories of "no postsecondary" and "mixed postsecondary": These occupations mostly require a high school diploma, but some jobholders have postsecondary credentials, such as an associate degree. *More education* refers to our previous categories of "postsecondary" and "mixed baccalaureate": They require a postsecondary degree, but some jobholders have baccalaureate credentials.

We generate these comparisons for each domain within O*NET. By taking the average, we are looking for elements that are ranked as important across all or most of the occupations. An element that may be very important to one occupation but not to others, such as an occupation-specific skill, will not rank highly through this method because the lower importance scores for the majority of occupations will drive its average down.

The Capability Needs of the Goal Occupations: Knowledge, Skills, and Abilities

The traditional domains within O*NET that are associated with education and training investments are the KSAs—knowledge, skills, and abilities. These domains span what a person needs to know and do in order to perform a job. These domains should also be the most teachable, and, from the ChalleNGe point of view, the easiest to adapt to the classroom setting. Within each KSA domain, we compare the top ten average elements in the goal occupations and all subbaccalaureate occupations and compare goal occupations that require more or less education.

Knowledge

Knowledge is defined as "organized sets of principles and facts applying in general domains" (O*NET OnLine, undated-b). Unlike most other O*NET categories, the 33 elements within Knowledge are not placed into subgroups. Elements include topic areas of knowledge such as Biology, Administration and Management, Food Production, Psychology, Transportation, and others. See Table C.2 in Appendix C for a full list of elements within Knowledge.

In Table 5.1, we show the top ten knowledge elements, by importance, among the goal occupations (left) and all subbaccalaureate occupations, goal and nongoal (right). In the middle, we show the average importance of the element among the two occupation groups. The elements are sorted by the average and ranked next to each other so that the table can show, first, which elements are most important *within* each group of occupations and, second, how relatively important they are *across* the groups. We present the data this way because we cannot assume that each domain will have important elements. The top ten ranked elements could average a score equivalent to "not important" or "somewhat important." Showing both rank and score helps us identify any absolutely and any comparatively more important elements. We color code each element to compare across the two groups, but the colors themselves are not meaningful.

Important across all subbaccalaureate occupations are English language and customer and personal service. More important for the goal occupations is computers and electronics. Note that the score of the remaining knowledge elements is below 3.0 (which we demarcate with a red line), meaning that on average they rated below "important." Although there are remaining differences between goal occupations and all subbaccalaureate occupations, since they are not ranked as important, we do not put a high weight on them.

In Table 5.2, we differentiate the top ten knowledge elements within the goal occupations by whether those occupations require less or more within the subbaccalaureate attainment level. Again, English language, customer

TABLE 5.1

Top Ten Knowledge Elements Rated Important, Goal Occupations and All Subbaccalaureate Occupations

	All Goal Occupations	Importance Score	All Subbaccalaureate Occupations	
Rank	Element		Element	Rank
1	English language	3.53		
2	Customer and personal service	3.48		
		3.36	English language	1
		3.36	Customer and personal service	2
3	Mathematics	3.12		
4	Computers and electronics	3.00		
		2.96	Mathematics	3
5	Public safety and security	2.93		
6	Mechanical	2.93		
7	Education and training	2.86		
		2.83	Administration and management	4
		2.82	Public safety and security	5
8	Administration and management	2.82		
		2.77	Education and training	6
		2.73	Mechanical	7
9	Clerical	2.73		
		2.69	Computers and electronics	8
10	Engineering and technology	2.65		
		2.63	Production and processing	9
		2.56	Clerical	10

SOURCES: Authors' analysis of O*NET, CPS, and EP data.

NOTES: This table ranks the elements within the domain of abilities in the O*NET by how important they are to an occupation within the goal occupations and the subbaccalaureate occupations. Importance score is the average among occupation groups in Likert-rated importance of that element to an occupation. Scores of 3.00 or above are considered "important."

and personal service, and mathematics knowledge are very important to both. Computer and electronics knowledge is more important to the more-education goal occupations, while mechanical and public safety and security knowledge are more important to the less-education goal occupations. And again, many of the top-ten elements are not important (below the red demarcation line).

TABLE 5.2

Top Ten Knowledge Elements Rated Important, Goal Occupations, by Education Level Within Subbaccalaureate Attainment

	Less-Education Goal Occupations	Importance	More-Education Goal Occupations	
Rank	Element	Score	Element	Rank
		3.69	English language	1
		3.49	Customer and personal service	2
1	Customer and personal service	3.48		
		3.41	Computers and electronics	3
2	English language	3.40		
		3.19	Mathematics	4
3	Mechanical	3.18		
4	Public safety and security	3.10		
5	Mathematics	3.07		
		2.93	Education and training	5
6	Administration and management	2.91		
		2.88	Clerical	6
		2.84	Engineering and technology	7
7	Education and training	2.81		
		2.73	Public safety and security	8
8	Building and construction	2.73		
		2.71	Administration and management	9
9	Computers and electronics	2.66		
		2.62	Mechanical	10
10	Clerical	2.60		

SOURCES: Authors' analysis of O*NET, CPS, and EP data.

NOTES: This table ranks the elements within the domain of abilities in the O*NET by how important they are to an occupation within the goal occupations that require definitely high school and mixed postsecondary versus definitely postsecondary with mixed baccalaureate. Importance score is the average among occupation groups in Likert-rated importance of that element to an occupation.

ChalleNGe Investments

For the ChalleNGe program, we are hoping to identify trainable or teachable investments that can be incorporated into the classroom setting or as part of the residential program. Many knowledge areas in Tables 5.1 and 5.2 do not average to be that important in absolute terms, and those that do, such as English and mathematics, are already integral to the ChalleNGe curriculum. In addition, because ChalleNGe is a quasi-military program, many aspects of public safety and security are part of the program ethos. We identify three knowledge elements that are ranked higher for goal occupations, score high enough to be relevant, and are not already part of ChalleNGe:

- computers and electronics
- mechanical
- customer and personal service.

Skills

Skills are defined as "developed capacities that facilitate learning or the more rapid acquisition of knowledge" (O*NET OnLine, undated-c). Skills elements are placed in six subgroups: basic skills, complex problem solving, resource management, social skills, systems skills, and technical skills. Definitions of each subgroup and specific elements under these each can be found in Table C.3 in Appendix C.

In Table 5.3, we show the top ten skills elements for the goal occupations and all subbaccalaureate occupations. There are five that are very important to both, though higher in absolute importance to the goal occupations: active listening, critical thinking, speaking, reading comprehension, and monitoring. But there are four additional skills among the goal occupations that average too low to be considered important for the average subbaccalaureate occupation: judgment and decision making, complex problem solving, time management, and coordination.

In Table 5.4, we differentiate the top ten skills elements within the goal occupations by whether those occupations require less or more within subbaccalaureate. Again, active listening, critical thinking, reading comprehension, and monitoring are important for both. More-education occupations also value writing and active learning. All of the elements across both groups rate in absolute terms as important, with the exception of operations monitoring.

ChalleNGe Investments

Comparing the goal occupations with all subbaccalaureate occupations, we do not find that the important skills vary much—the same skills were ranked and scored highly for all the occupations. Three of these skills in

TABLE 5.3

Top Ten Skills Elements Rated Important, Goal Occupations and All Subbaccalaureate Occupations

	All Goal Occupations	Importance Score	All Subbaccalaureate Occupations	
Rank	Element		Element	Rank
1	Active listening	3.47		
2	Critical thinking	3.45		
		3.37	Active listening	1
3	Speaking	3.36		
4	Reading comprehension	3.32		
		3.30	Speaking	2
		3.28	Critical thinking	3
5	Monitoring	3.17		
		3.16	Monitoring	4
		3.14	Reading comprehension	5
6	Judgment and decision making	3.11		
7	Complex problem solving	3.10		
8	Time management	3.03		
9	Coordination	3.03		
		3.02	Judgment and decision making	6
		3.01	Coordination	7
10	Social perceptiveness	2.99		
		2.99	Social perceptiveness	8
		2.98	Time management	9
		2.94	Complex problem solving	10

SOURCES: Authors' analysis of O*NET, CPS, and EP data.

NOTES: This table ranks the elements within the domain of abilities in the O*NET by how important they are to an occupation within the goal occupations and the subbaccalaureate occupations. Importance score is the average among occupation groups in Likert-rated importance of that element to an occupation.

particular are ranked highly by all occupations within the subbaccalaureate category:

- critical thinking
- active listening
- speaking.

The remainder are important, especially among the more-education goal occupations. Only one—reading comprehension—do we consider to

TABLE 5.4

Top Ten Skills Elements Rated Important, Goal Occupations, by Education Level Within Subbaccalaureate

	Less-Education Goal Occupations	Importance Score	More-Education Goal Occupations	
Rank	Element		Element	Rank
		3.66	Active listening	1
		3.60	Reading comprehension	2
		3.58	Critical thinking	3
		3.48	Speaking	4
1	Critical thinking	3.34		
2	Active listening	3.32		
		3.29	Monitoring	5
3	Speaking	3.26		
		3.24	Writing	6
		3.19	Complex problem solving	7
		3.17	Judgment and decision making	8
		3.11	Active learning	9
4	Reading comprehension	3.09		
5	Monitoring	3.08		
		3.08	Social perceptiveness	10
6	Judgment and decision making	3.06		
7	Complex problem solving	3.02		
8	Coordination	3.02		
9	Time management	3.01		
10	Operations monitoring	2.92		

SOURCES: Authors' analysis of O*NET, CPS, and EP data.

NOTES: This table ranks the elements within the domain of abilities in the O*NET by how important they are to an occupation within the goal occupations that require definitely high school and mixed postsecondary versus definitely postsecondary with mixed baccalaureate. Importance score is the average among occupation groups in Likert-rated importance of that element to an occupation.

be a part of the current ChalleNGe curriculum. Although these skills are not necessarily different or unique to the goal occupations, their ubiquity is reason to consider them good investments:

- monitoring
- complex problem solving
- judgment and decision making
- active learning
- writing.

Abilities

Abilities are defined as "enduring attributes of the individual that influence performance" (O*NET OnLine, undated-a). Abilities elements fall into four subgroups: cognitive abilities, physical abilities, psychomotor abilities, and sensory abilities. Definitions of each subgroup and specific elements under these each can be found in Table C.1 in Appendix C.

In Table 5.5, we show the top ten abilities elements by importance among the goal occupations (left) and all subbaccalaureate occupations, goal and

TABLE 5.5

Top Ten Abilities Elements Rated Important, Goal Occupations and All Subbaccalaureate Occupations

	All Goal Occupations	Importance Score	All Subbaccalaureate Occupations	
Rank	Element		Element	Rank
1	Near vision	3.66		
2	Oral comprehension	3.65		
3	Problem sensitivity	3.62		
4	Oral expression	3.56		
		3.54	Near vision	1
		3.53	Oral comprehension	2
		3.47	Oral expression	3
		3.47	Problem sensitivity	4
5	Deductive reasoning	3.43		
6	Written comprehension	3.41		
7	Information ordering	3.37		
8	Inductive reasoning	3.35		
9	Speech recognition	3.27		
		3.26	Deductive reasoning	5
10	Speech clarity	3.25		
		3.24	Speech recognition	6
		3.23	Information ordering	7
		3.22	Speech clarity	8
		3.21	Written comprehension	9
		3.16	Inductive reasoning	10

SOURCES: Authors' analysis of O*NET, CPS, and EP data.
NOTES: This table ranks the elements within the domain of abilities in the O*NET by how important they are to an occupation within the goal occupations and the subbaccalaureate occupations. Importance score is the average among occupation groups in Likert-rated importance of that element to an occupation.

nongoal (right). The same ten elements are in the top ten of importance for both groups, but three are ranked higher among the goal occupations: problem sensitivity (cognitive), written comprehension (cognitive), and inductive reasoning (cognitive). In addition, all elements score higher among the goal occupations. Near vision and speech recognition are sensory abilities; they are not teachable, so we do not discuss them.

In Table 5.6, we show the goal occupations only, this time comparing them by education level within subbaccalaureate. Breaking up the goal occupations by their education levels shows that the more-education occupations require more cognitive abilities. Oral comprehension, oral expression, written comprehension, and problem sensitivity (as well as near vision) all outscore in importance any ability from the less-education occupations. Further, the less-education occupations rank in importance psychomotor abilities, such as arm-hand steadiness, manual dexterity, and finger dexterity.

ChalleNGe Investments

Certain abilities, like near vision, speech clarity, and speech recognition, are not teachable. But from Tables 5.5 and 5.6, we identify several elements associated with the goal occupations and more-education goal occupations that could be incorporated into ChalleNGe. We list them here:

- oral comprehension
- oral expression
- written comprehension
- written expression
- inductive reasoning
- deductive reasoning
- information ordering.

The Environment of the Goal Occupations: Work Activities, Work Styles, and Work Context

Knowledge, skills, and abilities together describe what a worker needs in order to be *capable* of doing a job. The O*NET includes three domains that

TABLE 5.6

Top Ten Abilities Elements Rated Important, Goal Occupations, by Education Level Within Subbaccalaureate

	Less-Education Goal Occupations	Importance Score	More-Education Goal Occupations	
Rank	Element		Element	Rank
		3.85	Oral comprehension	1
		3.74	Oral expression	2
		3.73	Near vision	3
		3.71	Written comprehension	4
		3.70	Problem sensitivity	5
1	Near vision	3.61		
		3.57	Deductive reasoning	6
2	Problem sensitivity	3.55		
		3.49	Inductive reasoning	7
3	Oral comprehension	3.48		
		3.46	Information ordering	8
4	Oral expression	3.40		
		3.40	Written expression	9
		3.36	Speech clarity	10
		3.36	Speech recognition	11
5	Deductive reasoning	3.32		
6	Information ordering	3.29		
7	Inductive reasoning	3.24		
8	Speech recognition	3.20		
9	Arm-hand steadiness	3.18		
10	Manual dexterity	3.16		
11	Finger dexterity	3.16		

SOURCES: Authors' analysis of O*NET, CPS, and EP data.

NOTES: This table ranks the elements within the domain of abilities in the O*NET by how important they are to an occupation within the goal occupations that require definitely high school and mixed postsecondary versus definitely postsecondary with mixed baccalaureate. Importance score is the average among occupation groups in Likert-rated importance of that element to an occupation.

describe what a worker *does* on the job and what that job is like. These are not necessarily teachable or academic the way that knowledge, skills, and abilities are. However, given that ChalleNGe is more than an education program, these environmental elements merit inclusion.

Work Activities

Work activities are defined as "general types of job behaviors occurring on multiple jobs" (O*NET OnLine, undated-e). Elements within work activities fall into four subgroups: information input, interacting with others, mental processes, and work output. Definitions of each subgroup and specific elements under these each can be found in Table C.4 in Appendix C.

In Table 5.7, we compare the top ten work activities elements. All subbaccalaureate occupations rank the following as important: getting information; communicating with supervisors, peers, and subordinates; making decisions and solving problems; and identifying objects, actions, and events. After those top four, the goal occupations rank higher: updating and using relevant knowledge, documenting/recording information, evaluating information to determine compliance with standards, and processing information.

In Table 5.8, we differentiate the top ten work activities elements within the goal occupations by whether those occupations require less or more education within the subbaccalaureate attainment level. There is a larger difference between the less- and more-education goal occupations than there is between the goal and total subbaccalaureate occupations in terms of ranking and composition. The occupations with more education rank as follows: interacting with computers; evaluating information to determine compliance with standards; identifying objects, actions, and events; and processing information— four elements that are not part of the less-education goal occupation rankings.

ChalleNGe Notes

From Tables 5.7 and 5.8, there are six elements that score in absolute terms above (or very near) a 4.0. within the goal occupations, meaning that performing these activities well is, on average, very important to the job. These activities can be incorporated into ChalleNGe both in and out of the classroom setting. For that reason, we add them to the investment list:

- getting information
- interacting with computers
- communicating with supervisors, peers, and subordinates
- documenting/recording information
- making decisions and solving problems
- updating and using relevant knowledge.

TABLE 5.7

Top Ten Work Activities Elements Rated Important, Goal Occupations and All Subbaccalaureate Occupations

	All Goal Occupations	Importance Score	All Subbaccalaureate Occupations	
Rank	Element		Element	Rank
1	Getting information	4.21		
		4.07	Getting information	1
2	Communicating with supervisors, peers, or subordinates	3.97		
3	Making decisions and solving problems	3.93		
		3.85	Communicating with supervisors, peers, or subordinates	2
4	Identifying objects, actions, and events	3.84		
		3.75	Making decisions and solving problems	3
5	Updating and using relevant knowledge	3.75		
		3.74	Identifying objects, actions, and events	4
6	Documenting/recording information	3.65		
7	Evaluating information to determine compliance with standards	3.64		
8	Monitor processes, materials, or surroundings	3.63		
9	Organizing, planning, and prioritizing work	3.61		
		3.57	Monitor processes, materials, or surroundings	5
10	Processing information	3.57		
		3.50	Updating and using relevant knowledge	6
		3.50	Inspecting equipment, structures, or material	7
		3.47	Organizing, planning, and prioritizing work	8
		3.47	Establishing and maintaining interpersonal relationships	9
		3.43	Evaluating information to determine compliance with standards	10

SOURCES: Authors' analysis of O*NET, CPS, and EP data.

NOTES: This table ranks the elements within the domain of abilities in the O*NET by how important they are to an occupation within the goal occupations and the subbaccalaureate occupations. Importance score is the average among occupation groups in Likert-rated importance of that element to an occupation.

Work Styles

Work styles is defined by O*NET as "personal characteristics that can affect how well someone performs a job" (O*NET OnLine, undated-g). See

TABLE 5.8

Top Ten Work Activities Elements Rated Important, Goal Occupations, by Education Level Within Subbaccalaureate

	Less-Education Goal Occupations	Importance Score	More-Education Goal Occupations	
Rank	Element		Element	Rank
		4.31	Getting information	1
		4.16	Interacting with computers	2
1	Getting information	4.12		
		4.12	Communicating with supervisors, peers, or subordinates	3
		4.08	Documenting/recording information	4
		3.99	Making decisions and solving problems	5
		3.98	Updating and using relevant knowledge	6
		3.89	Identifying objects, actions, and events	7
2	Making decisions and solving problems	3.87		
3	Communicating with supervisors, peers, or subordinates	3.84		
		3.80	Evaluating information to determine compliance with standards	8
		3.79	Processing information	9
4	Identifying objects, actions, and events	3.79		
		3.74	Organizing, planning, and prioritizing work	10
5	Inspecting equipment, structures, or material	3.64		
6	Monitor processes, materials, or surroundings	3.58		
7	Updating and using relevant knowledge	3.56		
8	Handling and moving objects	3.52		
9	Organizing, planning, and prioritizing work	3.51		
10	Performing general physical activities	3.50		

SOURCES: Authors' analysis of O*NET, CPS, and EP data.
NOTES: This table ranks the elements within the domain of abilities in the O*NET by how important they are to an occupation within the goal occupations that require definitely high school and mixed postsecondary versus definitely postsecondary with mixed baccalaureate. Importance score is the average among occupation groups in Likert-rated importance of that element to an occupation.

Table C.5 in Appendix C for a full list of elements within work styles. In Tables 5.9 and 5.10, we compare the top ten work styles elements in the goal occupations with all subbaccalaureate occupations, as well as within goal occupations by education level. As the definition implies, these are personality traits and characteristics that are important in performing a job. We present them here because many of the elements align with ChalleNGe's

TABLE 5.9

Top Ten Work Styles Elements Rated Important, Goal Occupations and All Subbaccalaureate Occupations

	All Goal Occupations		Importance Score	All Subbaccalaureate Occupations	
Rank	Element			Element	Rank
1	Attention to detail		4.49		
2	Dependability		4.41		
			4.36	Attention to detail	1
			4.36	Dependability	2
3	Integrity		4.29		
			4.17	Integrity	3
4	Cooperation		4.11		
			4.07	Cooperation	4
5	Self control		4.02		
			4.01	Self control	5
6	Initiative		3.96		
7	Stress tolerance		3.95		
8	Adaptability/flexibility		3.94		
			3.90	Stress tolerance	6
9	Independence		3.88		
			3.87	Adaptability/flexibility	7
			3.87	Initiative	8
10	Persistence		3.85		
			3.83	Independence	9
			3.74	Persistence	10

SOURCES: Authors' analysis of O*NET, CPS, and EP data.
NOTES: This table ranks the elements within the domain of abilities in the O*NET by how important they are to an occupation within the goal occupations and the subbaccalaureate occupations. Importance score is the average among occupation groups in Likert-rated importance of that element to an occupation.

eight core components. The top ten elements in the goal occupations include attention to detail, dependability, integrity, cooperation, self-control, stress tolerance, adaptability/flexibility, persistence, independence, and initiative.

In Table 5.10, when comparing work styles by education within the goal occupations, we find that the same ten elements are rated as important for both education levels, with the exception of persistence. Among goal occupations with more education, analytical thinking is more important than persistence. Note, in the table, just how important these styles are. The

TABLE 5.10

Top Ten Work Styles Elements Rated Important, Goal Occupations, by Education Level Within Subbaccalaureate

	Less-Education Goal Occupations	Importance Score	More-Education Goal Occupations	
Rank	Element		Element	Rank
		4.59	Attention to detail	1
		4.46	Dependability	2
1	Attention to detail	4.42		
		4.41	Integrity	3
2	Dependability	4.37		
		4.21	Cooperation	4
3	Integrity	4.19		
		4.08	Adaptability/flexibility	5
		4.05	Self control	6
		4.02	Initiative	7
		4.02	Stress tolerance	8
4	Cooperation	4.02		
5	Self control	3.99		
		3.99	Analytical thinking	9
		3.94	Independence	10
6	Initiative	3.91		
7	Stress tolerance	3.88		
8	Independence	3.83		
9	Persistence	3.82		
10	Adaptability/flexibility	3.82		

SOURCES: Authors' analysis of O*NET, CPS, and EP data.

NOTES: This table ranks the elements within the domain of abilities in the O*NET by how important they are to an occupation within the goal occupations that require definitely high school and mixed postsecondary versus definitely postsecondary with mixed baccalaureate. Importance score is the average among occupation groups in Likert-rated importance of that element to an occupation.

average for attention to detail is 4.42 and 4.59; it falls between "very" and "extremely" important. Dependability and integrity fall into the same range for both groups as well.

ChalleNGe Notes

ChalleNGe programs make many investments in cadets outside the classroom as they build character through the eight core components. Those aims overlap with work style elements that are shown to be important among goal occupations. Since they are all scored highly (the lowest among goal occupations is 3.82), we list them all here:

- attention to detail
- dependability
- integrity
- cooperation
- self-control
- initiative
- stress tolerance
- independence
- persistence
- adaptability/flexibility.

Work Context

Work context is defined as "physical and social factors that influence the nature of work" (O*NET OnLine, undated-f). Specific elements under these four categories can be found in Table C.5 in Appendix C. Unlike all of the domains we have discussed so far, work context is not rated solely in terms of importance but also in terms of frequency. Its elements are ranked by how often a job requires that element (1—"Never," 2—"Once a year or more but not every month," 3—"Once a month or more but not every week," 4—"Once a week but not every day," 5—"Every day"). They also have question-specific scales, such as quantity (e.g., of hours in a work week or of emails).

At least weekly, the goal occupations include face-to-face discussions, contact with others, and the telephone; rated as very important is work with group or team; and there is a high degree of freedom to make decisions (Table 5.11).

In Table 5.12, we compare the goal occupations by education level within the subbaccalaureate attainment level. The less-education goal occupations have the same weekly elements, but the more-education goal occupations add indoor climate-controlled environment and electronic mail.

TABLE 5.11

Top Ten Work Context Elements Rated Frequent, Goal Occupations and All Subbaccalaureate Occupations

	All Goal Occupations	Frequency/ Importance Score	All Subbaccalaureate Occupations	
Rank	Element		Element	Rank
1	Face-to-face discussions	4.63		
		4.51	Face-to-face discussions	1
2	Importance of being exact or accurate	4.37		
3	Contact with others	4.37		
4	Telephone	4.32		
		4.30	Contact with others	2
		4.21	Importance of being exact or accurate	3
5	Work with work group or team	4.18		
		4.10	Work with work group or team	4
6	Freedom to make decisions	4.08		
7	Time pressure	3.98		
		3.97	Freedom to make decisions	5
8	Structured versus unstructured work	3.93		
9	Frequency of decision making	3.93		
		3.89	Telephone	6
10	Impact of decisions on co-workers or company results	3.89		
		3.87	Time pressure	7
		3.85	Structured versus unstructured work	8
		3.84	Frequency of decision making	9
		3.83	Spend time using your hands to handle, control, or feel objects, tools, or controls	10

SOURCES: Authors' analysis of O*NET, CPS, and EP data.

NOTES: This table ranks the elements within the domain of abilities in the O*NET by how important they are to an occupation within the goal occupations and the subbaccalaureate occupations. Frequency/importance score is the average among occupation groups in Likert-rated importance of that element to an occupation.

TABLE 5.12

Top Ten Work Context Elements Rated Frequent, Goal Occupations, by Education Level Within Subbaccalaureate

	Less-Education Goal Occupations		Frequency/ Importance Score	More-Education Goal Occupations	
Rank	Element			Element	Rank
			4.70	Face-to-face discussions	1
1	Face-to-face discussions		4.56		
			4.51	Indoors, environmentally controlled	2
			4.50	Importance of being exact or accurate	3
			4.43	Telephone	4
			4.40	Electronic mail	5
2	Contact with others		4.38		
			4.37	Contact with others	6
			4.29	Work with work group or team	7
3	Importance of being exact or accurate		4.27		
4	Telephone		4.23		
5	Freedom to make decisions		4.09		
6	Work with work group or team		4.09		
			4.06	Freedom to make decisions	8
7	Spend time using your hands to handle, control, or feel objects, tools, or controls		4.06		
8	Time pressure		4.01		
9	Frequency of decision making		3.98		
10	Structured versus unstructured work		3.95		
			3.94	Time pressure	9
			3.91	Structured versus unstructured work	10

SOURCES: Authors' analysis of O*NET, CPS, and EP data.

NOTES: This table ranks the elements within the domain of abilities in the O*NET by how important they are to an occupation within the goal occupations that require definitely high school and mixed postsecondary versus definitely postsecondary with mixed baccalaureate. Score is the average among occupation groups in Likert-rated importance of that element to an occupation.

ChalleNGe Notes

The work context elements give insight into the environment of these occupations. As with the other work domains, these are not necessarily teachable skills, but they do complement the skills we identified previously and give insight into what workers are expected to manage or perform for their jobs. We include the following in this list:

- face-to-face discussions
- importance of being exact or accurate
- contact with others
- telephone
- work with group or team
- freedom to make decisions.

The Investment List

In Table 5.13, we give an accounting of the investment list we have identified from the specific domains previously in the chapter. For four domains (knowledge, skills, abilities, and work activities), the table lists the element, the domain it is from, and the definition according to O*NET, and provides examples of the element. While KSAs are classic occupation components, *work activities* are somewhat an amalgamation of the prior three. An individual's work activities are determined by their capability, which itself is encompassed by KSAs of the worker. For each element, we give a definition and work-relevant examples of a low level and a medium level of that element. We omit the high level from the table because it was often too advanced to be helpful (e.g., design and teach an economics undergraduate course). Given that to qualify for the lists, the elements had to be important in performing the occupation, a worker should aim to be at the medium skill level. This table can provide a reference for site directors in thinking about how the elements translate to a workplace setting.

Work styles and *work context* do not have the same level of definitional detail as the other four domains but are also much more accessible and straightforward. *Work styles* are personality traits that enable a worker to be successful at a job; as such, there is not a low- or medium-level example. Rather than include them in the table, we list them here for completeness: attention to detail, dependability, integrity, cooperation, self-control, initiative, stress tolerance, independence, persistence, and adaptability/flexibility. *Work context* spans the physical and social factors that influence the job and

TABLE 5.13

High-Ranking Elements from Knowledge, Skills, Abilities, and Work Activities Domains of O*NET Among Goal Occupations

Element	Definition	Example—Low Level	Example—Medium Level
Knowledge domain			
Computers and electronics	Knowledge of circuit boards, processors, chips, electronic equipment, and computer hardware and software, including applications and programming	Operate a VCR/DVD player or use word processing software	Write a program to scan for viruses
Mechanical	Knowledge of machines and tools, including their designs, uses, repair, and maintenance	Replace the filters in a furnace	Replace a valve on a steam pipe
Customer and personal service	Knowledge of principles and processes for providing customer and personal services; this includes customer needs assessment, meeting quality standards for services, and evaluation of customer satisfaction	Process customer dry cleaning drop-off	Work as a day care aid supervising ten children; respond to a citizen's request for assistance after a disaster
Skills domain			
Critical thinking	Using logic and reasoning to identify the strengths and weaknesses of alternative solutions, conclusions, or approaches to problems	Determine whether a subordinate has a good excuse for being late	Evaluate a customer complaint and determine the appropriate response
Active listening	Giving full attention to what other people are saying, taking time to understand the points being made, asking questions as appropriate, and not interrupting at inappropriate times	Take a customer's order	Answer inquiries regarding credit inquiries
Speaking	Talking to others to convey information effectively	Greet tourists and explain tourist attractions	Interview applicants to obtain personal and work history

Table 5.13—Continued

Element	Definition	Example—Low Level	Example—Medium Level
Monitoring	Monitoring/assessing performance of yourself, other individuals, or organizations to make improvements or take corrective action	Proofread and correct a letter	Monitor a meeting's progress and revise the agenda to ensure that important topics are discussed
Complex problem solving	Identifying complex problems and reviewing related information to develop and evaluate options and implement solutions	Lay out tools to complete a job	Redesign a floor layout to take advantage of new manufacturing techniques
Judgment and decision making	Considering the relative costs and benefits of potential actions to choose the most appropriate one	Decide how scheduling a break will affect work flow	Evaluate a loan application for degree of risk
Active learning	Understanding the implications of new information for both current and future problem-solving and decisionmaking	Think about the implications of a newspaper article for job opportunities	Determine the impact of new menu changes on a restaurant's purchasing requirements
Writing	Communicating effectively in writing as appropriate for the needs of the audience	Take a telephone message	Write a novel
Abilities domain			
Oral comprehension	The ability to listen to and understand information and ideas presented through spoken words and sentences	Understand a television commercial	Understand a coach's oral instructions for a sport
Oral expression	The ability to communicate information and ideas in speaking so that others will understand	Cancel a reservation or subscription over the phone	Give instructions to a lost driver
Written comprehension	The ability to read and understand information and ideas presented in writing	Understand highway signs	Understand an apartment lease

Table 5.13—Continued

Element	Definition	Example—Low Level	Example—Medium Level
Written expression	The ability to communicate information and ideas in writing so that others will understand	Leave a note to remind someone to take food out of the freezer	Write a job recommendation for a subordinate
Inductive reasoning	The ability to combine pieces of information to form general rules or conclusions (includes finding a relationship among seemingly unrelated events)	Decide what to wear based on the weather report	Determine the prime suspect based on crime scene evidence
Deductive reasoning	The ability to apply general rules to specific problems to produce answers that make sense	Know that a stalled car can coast downhill	Decide what factors to consider when buying stocks
Information ordering	The ability to arrange things or actions in a certain order or pattern according to a specific rule or set of rules (e.g., patterns of numbers, letters, words, pictures, mathematical operations)	Put things in numerical order	Assemble equipment based on instructions
Work activities domain			
Getting information	Observing, receiving, and otherwise obtaining information from all relevant sources	Follow a standard blueprint	Review a budget
Interacting with computers	Using computers and computer systems (including hardware and software) to program, write software, set up functions, enter data, or process information	Enter employee information into a computer database	Write software for keeping track of parts in inventory
Communicating with supervisors, peers, and subordinates	Providing information to supervisors, coworkers, and subordinates by telephone, in written form, e-mail, or in person	Write brief notes to others	Report the results of a sales meeting to a supervisor

Table 5.13—Continued

Element	Definition	Example—Low Level	Example—Medium Level
Documenting/ recording information	Entering, transcribing, recording, storing, or maintaining information in written or electronic/magnetic form	Record the weights of trucks that use the highways	Document the results of a crime scene investigation
Making decisions and solving problems	Analyzing information and evaluating results to choose the best solution and solve problems	Determine the meal selection for a cafeteria	Select the location for a major department store
Updating and using relevant knowledge	Keeping up-to-date technically and applying new knowledge to your job	Keep up with price changes in a small retail store	Keep current on changes in maintenance procedures for repairing sports cars

SOURCES: Authors' analysis of O*NET, CPS, and EP data.
NOTES: This table presents the elements from four O*NET domains, their definitions, and examples. Elements were selected for inclusion by their relative importance to goal occupations.

also do not require level examples: face-to-face discussions, importance of being exact or accurate, contact with others, telephone, work with group or team, and freedom to make decisions.

Our method had no guarantee of findings. We knew that we could identify goal occupations using the EP and the CPS and that we could compare goal and nongoal occupations in the O*NET. However, once we averaged out the occupation-specific skill and features, there was not a guarantee that the remaining elements would pattern around the occupation divisions that we made. It could have been the case that none of the elements averaged as important across all occupations. This is somewhat visible in the knowledge and abilities domains, where some of the highest-ranked elements were not important; their score averaged less than 3. But we identified commonly important elements across the six domains we examined. Hence, we have identified that there are multiple skill components in the middle-skills occupations, some of which are occupation-specific, and some of which are broad.

For most of the domains, the difference between goal occupations and the remaining subbaccalaureate occupations was the importance of the element (whether for a knowledge area or specific skill). Often the larger difference was seen when comparing within goal occupations by education level. For the most part, we added to our "investment list" the elements that met some minimum importance rating and were ranked as more important by goal occupations and more-education goal occupations. In some cases, an element was important to all groups, with few differences seen across groups, and we included the element in the investment list because it was broad and important overall. Our analysis produced a comprehensive investment list, which we discuss in more detail in the next chapter.

CHAPTER SIX

Finding 3—Current and Potential Investments That ChalleNGe Can Make in Skills and Capabilities for Cadets

The goal of this report is to provide ChalleNGe administrators and site directors with insights into the labor market that cadets will enter and how to help them prepare for it. Rather than proposing which occupation or occupations are the best to invest in, we deconstructed middle-skills goal occupations—those that met our criteria of being attainable, high-paying, and growth-oriented—into a set of skills. We then identified the skills that are shared across numerous occupations. This allows us to identify broad investments that sites can make to benefit all cadets while remaining afford-able within the bounds of the program.

While we focus the discussion below on ChalleNGe, the findings in this report provide guidance and suggestions for Job ChalleNGe programs, too, as staff at these programs work with their community partners to select the most-appropriate training programs for their participants, and as they schedule activities for participants during the periods of time not taken up by job training–related coursework. The Job ChalleNGe program is rela-tively new (the initial pilot program ended in late 2019). Consequently, the program is still making implementation decisions, so this information may be well-timed.

In analyzing the O*NET, we identified nearly 50 elements that were important to the goal occupations from the domains of KSAs, work activi-ties, work styles, and work contexts. Not all of these elements can be translated well to a classroom, however, and many overlap. In this chapter, we group these elements into themes to focus on how to make broad skill investments in the classroom. We first talk about areas where the elements identified overlap with the current ChalleNGe program, and then we discuss how ChalleNGe could incorporate more skills.

Investments That ChalleNGe Is Already Making

ChalleNGe is already making investments in helping cadets become productive citizens. The educational goal of ChalleNGe is to help cadets complete high school, whether that is through earning a GED or credit recovery. But education is only one part of ChalleNGe's eight core components: academic excellence, physical fitness, leadership/followership, responsible citizenship, job skills, service to community, health and hygiene, and life-coping skills.

We found in our analysis of occupations that many skills we identify as important to middle-skills goal occupations are already built into the ChalleNGe program. Math, English language, and reading comprehension are already part of the curriculum through classroom work. No doubt many instructors, principals, and site directors know that math and English skills will have dividends in the labor market—we merely affirm that with our analysis.

Another area that ChalleNGe invests in is the O*NET domain of work styles. A *work style* is a personal characteristic that affects how well someone does a job. It can also be thought of as encompassing traits that are not about *acquiring* skills, but *executing* them. We identified ten work styles elements among the goal occupations that ranged from very important to extremely important in performing a job. We present these traits and their definitions in Table 6.1.

Cadets exhibit many of these traits by participating in ChalleNGe, including initiative, independence, and adaptability/flexibility, as cadets must willingly leave the comforts of home for nearly half a year to seek out structure and reclaim their education. Further, many of these traits are built into the daily life of the program, such as attention to detail and cooperation, or are instilled as part of the program's goals, such as dependability,

TABLE 6.1

Work Style Elements Ranked as Very Important or Extremely Important Among Goal Occupations and Their Definitions

Work Style	Definition
Attention to detail	Job requires being careful about details and thorough in completing tasks
Dependability	Job requires being reliable, responsible, and dependable in fulfilling obligations
Integrity	Job requires being honest and ethical
Cooperation	Job requires being pleasant with others on the job and displaying a good-natured, cooperative attitude
Self-control	Job requires maintaining composure, keeping emotions in check, controlling anger, and avoiding aggressive behavior, even in very difficult situations
Initiative	Job requires a willingness to take on responsibilities and challenges
Stress tolerance	Job requires accepting criticism and dealing calmly and effectively with high-stress situations
Independence	Job requires developing one's own ways of doing things, guiding oneself with little or no supervision, and depending on oneself to get things done
Persistence	Job requires persistence in the face of obstacles
Adaptability/flexibility	Job requires being open to change (positive or negative) and to considerable variety in the workplace

NOTE: Definitions are from O*NET, undated.

integrity, self-control, and stress tolerance. Finally, no cadet can finish the rigor of the ChalleNGe program without persistence.

These traits are not just important to ChalleNGe but are an integral part of being a successful worker in the goal occupations we identify. Again, many ChalleNGe site directors, instructors, cadres, and recruiters already know this to be true, but we affirm this in our statistical analysis.

Skills in Which ChalleNGe Can Invest More

There are also areas in which ChalleNGe might consider building on its investment. We present the investment elements from O*NET (see Table 5.13 for KSAs, and activities and its discussion for styles and context) through six key skill investment areas. These areas are often related and sometimes overlapping in terms of the elements discussed. Our goal in grouping them was not to find mutually exclusive categories, but to think of how these elements might be translated into the ChalleNGe program.

1. Oral and Written Expression

Many of the important O*NET elements for the goal occupations center around oral and written communication and expression. For students at younger ages, and in preparation for high school exams, the focus is often on comprehension: Can a student understand what they have heard or what they have read? Oral and written comprehension are important skills (and were included on our investment list), but they are already included as part of the academic curriculum. The workplace demands that communication be a two-way street. Oral expression and written expression were both identified as important skills and abilities. Face-to-face discussions and communication over the telephone were reported to be at least weekly, but for some, daily parts of the job. Workers are expected to express themselves clearly and effectively.

The O*NET gives examples of these expression skills, such as writing a letter of recommendation for a subordinate, interviewing a job applicant, or giving directions to a lost driver. Simulations of these types of activities can be incorporated into the classroom or into extracurricular activities, or into any opportunity for cadets to practice articulating clearly.

2. Being on/Communicating with a Team

Related to oral and written expression, these important O*NET elements reflect a work environment that is team-based. Important work activities included communicating with supervisors, peers, and subordinates. Daily work activities include working on a team and being in direct contact with others. One key skill is active listening, which involves giving full attention to what other people are saying, processing what they say, and not interrupting. In the history of subbaccalaureate jobs, this type of professional communication has not always been a component. Many production occupations, for example, do not require group collaboration but rather successful execution of an assigned task or activity. But many of the goal occupations draw from fields in which teamwork and communication are key components, from the construction site to the hospital room.

Cadets are organized in platoons and build group cooperation and dependability skills as part of the shared responsibility of good behavior, and the program includes an explicit emphasis on leadership/followership. However, cadets could benefit from broader opportunities to work or solve problems in small groups. Given their wide academic backgrounds, cadets have a lot of independent work in the classroom. From a skills perspective, that is also a great investment, but one that can be complemented with small-team communication and practice.

3. Logic and Reasoning

Even among subbaccalaureate occupations, many workers rated basic logic, reasoning, and problem solving as important to the performance of their jobs. Critical thinking and complex problem solving are important skills, and inductive and deductive reasoning are important abilities. Work-based examples of these skills and abilities include determining the prime suspect based on crime scene evidence, redesigning a floor layout of a workshop or plant to take advantage of new techniques, or knowing that a stalled car can roll downhill. There are many ways to incorporate logic games, puzzles, even mysteries or crime novels into a cadet's repertoire while at ChalleNGe.

4. Information Expertise

In prior eras, many of the good subbaccalaureate jobs involved the handling of materials in production. While many of our goal occupations still require hands-on physical work, in many cases, the focus of many others is on producing information. Capturing, ordering, processing, and remembering information are key to many jobs. Important skills include *active learning*, which is defined as understanding the implications of new information. Important abilities include *information ordering*, or putting things or actions in a proper pattern or rule. Examples of *information expertise* would be reading an article in the newspaper and understanding whether it could affect which jobs to apply for, putting things in numerical order, assembling equipment based on instruction, following a blueprint, or making a budget. Further, important elements in work activities were getting information and documenting/recording information. In many ways, the fundamentals of academic preparation for finishing high school encompass information expertise. But, as with logic and reasoning, there are supplemental games, activities, or quizzes that could increase cadets' familiarity with information.

5. Decisionmaking

Using information, facts, and data to make decisions is an important element identified in the O*NET data among the goal occupations. Evaluating information to make decisions, whether making a judgment or solving a problem, is a part of good subbaccalaureate jobs, as is the weighing of costs and benefits of potential actions in selecting a course. As adults navigating the world, cadets will have to make decisions regularly in their daily lives. For workers, this skill can require concerted effort. It spans deciding the menu at a cafeteria, selecting the location of a store, deciding how a break will affect worker productivity, and evaluating a loan application for risk. Advice and experience are the biggest aids for making life decisions and judgments, but professional decisionmaking and judgment are a matter of learning how to weigh potential actions and information. Judgment and decisionmaking can be incorporated into ChalleNGe through role playing, games, stories, and book discussion, among many other activities.

6. Computer Familiarity

In both knowledge and activity, the use and understanding of computers is an important element of the goal occupations. The decision to incorporate technology into cadets' education can be a function of budget and resources, but many sites choose not to incorporate technology or computers because administrators feel that cadets will not use them in accordance with the rules and that firewalls or website blocks can be worked around. While this is a valid concern, cadets also need to be fluent with computers for many jobs and may not come from the income backgrounds to have sufficient exposure to computers and opportunities to practice at home. In particular, cadets need to learn proper and professional communication skills and apply them in the appropriate setting, such as how to email a supervisor or how to follow up with a job interview.

Signaling Skills and Investing Skills

We have presented potential skill investments that ChalleNGe site leaders can incorporate into their programs and curricula. We believe that these are good labor market investments, especially given their importance to attainable, growth-oriented, high-paying jobs. However, much of the labor market operates from signals of skill, which our suggested investments do not have. A high school diploma and a GED, for example, contain multiple signals. Both show a level of educational attainment, but the diploma signals that the person finished traditional high school, while the GED signals that the person did not. In many cases, the education credential could be more valuable as a signal of the person's background than of their skills or knowledge.

In all levels of the labor market, workers use prior experience, courses, certificates, and various credentials to signal—or demonstrate—the skills they have. It is a fair argument that a site may prefer to send cadets to training that provides a firm signal, such as a six-week course in food handling or certified nurse's assistant, rather than to distributed skill investments in classes. A site cannot easily signal that its cadets run a series of crime-solving games, and that each has worked to cultivate reasoning and logic skills in the process—and sites have limited resources. Another interpretation of our analyses is that many of the activities at ChalleNGe sites build skills that are rewarded in the job market. In other words, even activities that do not obviously link to a specific job or career can help to prepare cadets for the labor force.

Our findings are relevant for the Job ChalleNGe program, too. Job ChalleNGe has a strong and explicit emphasis on job training, but the program also includes activities that focus on all eight core components. Our findings here provide guidance for Job ChalleNGe as well. First, these findings reveal specific occupations that offer good wages and have a positive future outlook. But the skill investment findings also have implications for Job ChalleNGe; weaving activities through the program with a focus on developing relevant skills is another way of preparing participants for the job market.

Developing the skills we discuss generally does not result in an earned credential. Nonetheless, these are investments in skills and traits that should help cadets and Job ChalleNGe participants to succeed in a challenging and often changing labor market. These skills will support their success in any number of occupations or training programs and, thus, will help the ChalleNGe program to achieve its mission of improving the lives of young people.

Assessment of Occupation Families

In this appendix, we walk through the fourth step in our method of selecting goal occupations: assessment. Very few occupations meet all the numeric
criteria we establish of being attainable, high-paying, and growth oriented.
Moreover, the numeric factors are limited by what is included in data sets,
but there is much more information, such as the other "good jobs" lists that
are published. Hence, in this step, we assess each occupation's overall performance and select the goal occupations. We frame this assessment through
the lens of *occupation families*, which are groups of related occupations.

Occupation Families

We sort the 453 occupations in the CPS into a set of groups, which we call
families.[1] We present this information in Table A.1. Within each family, we
list the CPS titles and codes, number of occupations, and the number of
subbaccalaureate occupations (occupations in which at least two-thirds of
job holders have less than a bachelor's degree). The occupation families vary
in the share that are subbaccalaureate. Engineering, science, and technicians span 36 occupations, only seven of which are subbaccalaureate, while
food preparation and serving are all subbaccalaureate. We will discuss each
family, the share of subbaccalaureate occupations, and the performance of
those occupations under our criteria.

---

[1]   The CPS has defined occupational categories. Some of our families are a single CPS
category; others are multiple CPS categories combined. The notes under Table A.1 give
the specific category names in the CPS.

TABLE A.1

Introduction to Occupation Families

Occupation Family	Codes in CPS	Number of Occupations	Number of Subbaccalaureate Occupations	Examples of Subbaccalaureate Occupations
Management and business	950	46	11	Tax preparer, property/real estate/community association manager, claims adjuster
Computer and mathematical	1000 to 1240	10	3	Web developer, computer network/user support specialist, statistician
Engineering and science	1300 to 1980	36	7	Architectural/civil drafter, electrical/electronics drafter, mechanical drafter, surveying/mapping technician, geological/petroleum/nuclear technician
Legal and education	2000 to 2550	20	4	Community health worker, court reporter, library technician, teacher assistant
Arts, design, entertainment, sports and media	2600 to 2920	16	6	Audio/video equipment technician, broadcast technician, photographer, sound engineering technician
Health	3000 to 3650	35	17	Dental assistant, occupational therapy assistant, medical assistant, licensed practical and licensed vocational nurse

Table A.1—Continued

Occupation Family	Codes in CPS	Number of Occupations	Number of Subbaccalaureate Occupations	Examples of Subbaccalaureate Occupations
Protective service	3700 to 3950	13	13	Firefighter, correctional officer, security guard, animal control worker, transit and railroad police
Food preparation and serving	4000 to 4150	18	18	Bartender, cook/chef
Building and grounds cleaning and maintenance	4200 to 4250	6	6	Landscaping and groundskeeper, tree trimmer/pruner, pest control worker
Personal care and service	4300 to 4650	18	18	Personal care aide, animal trainer, barber, skincare specialist
Sales and related	4700 to 4965	17	17	Real estate broker/agent, travel agent, insurance sales agent, advertising sales agent
Office and administrative support	5000 to 5940	50	49	Customer service representative, medical secretary, legal secretary, information/record clerk
Construction	6200 to 6765	29	29	Carpenter, glazier, brickmason and blockmason, elevator installer and repairer
Extraction	6800 to 6940	5	5	Derrick operator, earth driller, rotary drill operator
Installation, maintenance, and repair	7000 to 7630	34	34	Avionics technician, wind turbine service technician, home appliance repairer

Table A.1—Continued

Occupation Family	Codes in CPS	Number of Occupations	Number of Subbaccalaureate Occupations	Examples of Subbaccalaureate Occupations
Production	7700 to 8965	71	71	Chemical plant and systems operator, baker, machinist, medical appliance technician
Transportation and material moving	9000 to 9750	29	29	Commercial pilot, air traffic controller, airfield operations specialist, ship engineer

SOURCE: Author compilations of BLS data.
NOTES: *Management* spans CPS categories Management in Business, Science and Arts; Business Operation Specialists; Financial Specialists. *Engineering and science* spans CPS categories Architecture and Engineering; Technicians; Life, Physical, and Social Sciences. *Legal and education* spans CPS categories Community and Social Services; Legal; Education, Training, and Library. *Health* spans CPS categories Healthcare Practitioners and Technicians and Healthcare Support.

Management and Business Occupations

The management and business occupations cover the range of occupations that "keep the lights on" in a company. Workers in these occupations play some role in running the business, whether managing people, logistics, or finances. These jobs are generally high-paying, but very few are held by workers without at least a four-year degree. Of the 63 management occupations, our education filter rules out all but 12. In Table A.2, we present the occupations that appear to be accessible to those without a four-year degree. Following left to right, the first three columns measure attainability: whether the job is easy to get (i.e., past experience is not required), whether the occupation grew in the number of jobs in the past business cycle, and whether it is projected to grow in the number of jobs. The next nine columns measure pay and show whether the job is high-paying for all workers and then each of the race-by-gender groups. Finally, the last column indicates whether the job is associated with OJT, either none (blank) or low (L), medium (M), or high (H).

Many of the subbaccalaureate occupations in management require previous related experience (column 1), meaning that they would be less accessible to younger, inexperienced workers. While these management occupations generally did not grow over the past decade, most are projected to

TABLE A.2
Management Occupations

Occupation	Easy to Get	Grew 2010–2018	Projected 2018–2028	All Workers	Black Men	Black Women	Hispanic Men	Hispanic Women	White Men	White Women	Other Men	Other Women	OJT
Transportation, storage, and distribution manager	N	N	Y	Y	Y	Y	Y	Y	Y	Y	Y	Y	
Farmer, rancher, and other Agricultural manager	N	Y	N	N	N	Y	N	N	N	Y	N	Y	
Food service and lodging managers	N	Y	Y	N	N	N	N	Y	N	N	Y	Y	
Funeral director	Y	Y	Y	Y	Y	Y	Y	Y	Y	Y	Y	Y	H
Gaming manager	N	N	Y	Y	Y	Y	Y	Y	Y	Y	Y	Y	
Property, real estate, and community association manager	N	Y	Y	Y	Y	Y	Y	Y	Y	Y	N	Y	
Buyer and purchasing agent, farm products		N	Y	Y	Y	Y	Y	Y	Y	Y	Y	Y	
Wholesale and retail buyer, except farm products		N	Y	Y	N	Y	N	Y	Y	Y	N	Y	

Table A.2—Continued

Occupation	Easy to Get	Grew 2010–2018	Projected 2018–2028	All Workers	Black Men	Black Women	Hispanic Men	Hispanic Women	White Men	White Women	Other Men	Other Women	OJT
Purchasing agent, except wholesale, retail, and farm products	Y	N	Y	Y	Y	Y	Y	Y	Y	Y	Y	Y	
Claims adjuster, appraiser, examiner, and investigator		Y	N	Y	N	Y	Y	Y	Y	Y	Y	Y	M/H
Tax preparer	Y	N	Y	Y	Y	Y	Y	Y	Y	Y	Y	Y	M

NOTES: 2010–2018 growth data and high-paying calculations are derived from the CPS. Projected growth and rating of the amount of OJT is from the BLS EP. Y = yes; N = no. OJT options are none (blank), low ("L"), moderate ("M"), and high ("H"). High-paying is calculated as being above the median wage for subbaccalaureate workers, both overall ("All") and by race/ethnic-gender interaction. *Easy to get* is an indicator for an occupation not requiring prior experience—it is a true entry-level occupation. A few occupations (e.g. buyer and purchasing agent) had too much internal variance to categorize their *easy to get* status. Goal occupations are shown in green cells in the first column.

grow over the next decade. And most occupations, outside of managerial positions related to food, paid higher wages for all the groups listed. However, few of these occupations appear growth-oriented in terms of career: Only two are classified as having any OJT, according to the BLS. Since the management occupations are associated with prior experience, OJT is an important component of our assessment of what are "good" management occupations. Hence, we classify only three occupations in this family as goal occupations: claims adjuster, appraiser, examiner, and investigator; funeral director; and tax preparer. We highlight these occupations in green.

Computer and Mathematical Occupations

Computer and mathematical occupations, which include information technology, make up half of the STEM occupations. Our education filter leaves us with just three subbaccalaureate occupations, which we show in Table A.3. All the occupations related to mathematics require at least a bachelor's degree, but occupations related to computing and technology are more varying. Computer and information technology is a quickly growing

TABLE A.3

Computer, Information Technology, and Mathematics Occupations

Occupation	Easy to Get	Grew 2010–2018	Projected 2018–2028	All Workers	Black Men	Black Women	Hispanic Men	Hispanic Women	White Men	White Women	Other Men	Other Women	OJT
Computer support specialist	Y	Y	Y	Y	Y	Y	Y	Y	Y	Y	Y	Y	
Statistician[a]	N	Y	N										
Web developer	Y	Y	Y	Y	Y	Y	Y		Y	Y	Y	Y	

NOTES: 2010–2018 growth data and high-paying calculations derived from the CPS. Projected growth and rating of the amount of OJT is from the BLS EP. Y = yes; N = no. OJT options are none (blank), low ("L"), moderate ("M"), and high ("H"). High-paying is calculated as being above the median wage for subbaccalaureate workers, both overall ("All") and by race/ethnic-gender interaction. *Easy to get* is an indicator for an occupation not requiring prior experience—it is a true entry-level occupation.

[a] Sample too small to perform subgroup wage analysis.

and evolving field. In the 1990s, for example, the CPS had only one occupation (computer systems analyst) in the computing and information technology fields; the next CPS will have more than a dozen. Many technical occupations, such as web developer, are accessible after short-term non-credential training bootcamps. While this is a short selection of occupations, they are fast-growing and high-paying. Although they do not have OJT, the field itself—meaning the number of occupations, not the number of jobs—is broadening, so we weigh OJT less here. Computer support specialists and web developers make our goal list. We do not select statistician because there is too much variation in how much training and experience is required—some have a Ph.D. in statistics, and some have only attended a bootcamp in data science.

Engineering and Science Occupations

The engineering and science occupations are the other half of STEM occupations (Table A.4). Like computer and math, most of these occupations require a high level of education (of the 36 occupations, only seven are sub-baccalaureate). However, unlike computer and math, most occupations in the sciences require technicians of some kind. These technician occupations require considerable training and are highly specialized in that training—it is not easy to switch jobs from, say, a drafter to a chemical technician. Yet, we recommend all the technician occupations for the sciences; they are high-paying, growing occupations and nearly all are associated with a medium (one to 12 months) level of OJT. The only occupation not expected to grow is drafter; however, we include it because it is not projected to decline over the next decade, and it pays well across each of our subgroups of interest.

Legal and Education Occupations

Similar to management and STEM occupations, the community, social services, legal, and education occupations generally require bachelor's or advanced degrees, but there are occupations in support roles that do not have such a requirement. Again, of the 20 occupations in this family, only four are subbaccalaureate, which we show in Table A.5. Although education and legal services support occupations are generally attainable, only the legal side pays well; library technician and teacher assistant positions are

TABLE A.5

Legal and Education Occupations

Occupation	Easy to Get	Grew 2010-2018	Projected 2018-2028	All Workers	Black Men	Black Women	Hispanic Men	Hispanic Women	White Men	White Women	Other Men	Other Women	OJT
Paralegals and legal assistant	Y	Y	Y	Y	Y	Y	Y	Y	Y	Y	Y	Y	
Legal support worker, not elsewhere classified	Y	N	Y	Y	Y	Y	Y	Y	Y	Y	Y	Y	L/M
Library technician	Y	Y	N	N	Y	Y	Y	Y	Y	Y	Y	Y	
Teacher assistant	Y	Y	Y	N	N	N	Y	N	N	N	Y	N	

NOTES: 2010–2018 growth data and high-paying calculations derived from the CPS. Projected growth and rating of the amount of OJT is from the BLS EP. Y = yes; N = no. OJT options are none (blank), low ("L"), moderate ("M"), and high ("H"). High-paying is calculated as being above the median wage for subbaccalaureate workers, both overall ("All") and by race/ethnic-gender interaction. *Easy to get* is an indicator for an occupation not requiring prior experience—it is a true entry-level occupation.

less well-compensated, and their jobs—potentially subject to public funding cuts—may be less secure. Hence, only paralegal, legal assistant, and legal support worker make the goal occupations list.

Arts, Design, Entertainment, Sports, and Media Occupations

Arts and related occupations (Table A.6) span the most famous professions but also both rapidly growing (e.g., film and sports) and rapidly declining (e.g., publishing) industries, which also tend to be geographically concentrated. There is a role for technicians, but otherwise the arts are a less–formally educated but highly competitive field. The occupations in this occupational family show the weakness in our approach, in that *attainability* should encompass "availability" or "plausibility" but does not here. Although being a photographer does not necessarily require higher education, it not advisable that a youth program such as ChalleNGe encourage all students to become photographers. For that reason, we focus our interest on

TABLE A.4

Engineering, Science, and Technician Occupations

Occupation	Easy to Get	Grew 2010–2018	Projected 2018–2028	All Workers	Black Men	Black Women	Hispanic Men	Hispanic Women	White Men	White Women	Other Men	Other Women	OJT
Drafter	Y	Y	N	Y	Y	Y	Y	Y	Y	Y	Y	Y	
Engineering technician, except drafter	Y	Y	Y	Y	Y	Y	Y	Y	Y	Y	Y	Y	
Surveying and mapping technician	Y	Y	Y	Y	Y	Y	Y	Y	Y	Y	Y	Y	M
Agricultural and food science technician	Y	Y	Y	Y	Y	Y	Y	Y	Y	Y	Y	Y	M
Chemical technician	Y	N	Y	Y	Y	Y	Y	Y	Y	Y	Y	Y	M
Geological and petroleum technician, and nuclear technician	Y	N	Y	Y	Y	Y	Y	Y	Y	Y	Y	Y	M
Life, physical, and social science technician	Y	Y	Y	Y	Y	Y	Y	Y	Y	Y	Y	N	M

NOTES: 2010–2018 growth data and high-paying calculations derived from the CPS. Projected growth and rating of the amount of OJT is from the BLS EP. Y = yes; N = no. OJT options are none (blank), low ("L"), moderate ("M"), and high ("H"). High-paying is calculated as being above the median wage for subbaccalaureate workers, both overall ("All") and by race/ethnic-gender interaction. *Easy to get* is an indicator for an occupation not requiring prior experience—it is a true entry-level occupation.

TABLE A.6

Arts and Entertainment Occupations

Occupation	Easy to Get	Grew 2010–2018	Projected 2018–2028	All Workers	Black Men	Black Women	Hispanic Men	Hispanic Women	White Men	White Women	Other Men	Other Women	OJT
Dancer and choreographer	N	Y	N	N	Y	Y	Y	Y	Y	N	Y	Y	H
Entertainer and performer, sports and related worker, all other	Y	Y	Y	N	Y	Y	Y	Y	Y	Y	Y	Y	L
Announcer	Y	N	N	Y	Y	Y	Y	Y	Y	Y	Y	Y	L
Media and communication worker, not elsewhere classified	Y	N	Y	Y	Y	Y	Y	Y	Y	N	Y	Y	L
Broadcast and sound engineering technician and radio operator, and media and communication equipment worker, all other	Y	N	Y	Y	N	Y	Y	Y	Y	Y	Y	Y	L
Photographer	Y	Y	N	N	Y	Y	Y	N	Y	N	Y	Y	M

NOTES: 2010–2018 growth data and high-paying calculations derived from the CPS. Projected growth and rating of the amount of OJT is from the BLS EP. Y = yes; N = no. OJT options are none (blank), low ("L"), moderate ("M"), and high ("H"). High-paying is calculated as being above the median wage for subbaccalaureate workers, both overall ("All") and by race/ethnic-gender interaction. *Easy to get* is an indicator for an occupation not requiring prior experience—it is a true entry-level occupation.

the more training-focused positions, such as the technicians, rather than the talent-focused positions. We add broadcast and sound engineering technician and radio operator to our goal occupations.

Health Occupations

Health (Table A.7) is a growing sector; these occupations are expected overall to add jobs at three times the rate of all other occupations (Salsberg and Martiniano, 2018). And unlike the previously discussed occupation families, only about half of health occupations require a bachelor's degree or higher. Indeed, the health occupations straddle the mostly high-education, high-skill occupation families that we have discussed so far, such as those in engineering, and the mostly low-education occupations that we will discuss next, such as food service. Health has both ends of education and, hence, both ends of wages. Indeed, unlike the STEM occupation families, there is more wage dispersion among health occupations. Low-education health occupations typically pay barely above minimum wage.

Given that health is one of the largest and fastest-growing occupational sectors, there is an argument to move all the health occupations to goal occupations, implying that *any* job in health is a good job. However, about a third of the subbaccalaureate health occupations are relatively low-paying. These jobs tend to be as assistants/aides rather than technicians. Examining the health occupational family, we can also begin to see that certain occupations are comparatively high-paying for members of minority groups, but not for white workers, reflecting inequality present in the subbaccalaureate labor market, as white subbaccalaureate workers make more in general than nonwhite subbaccalaureate workers. In selecting goal occupations, we kept all therapists and technicians, and we excluded all assistants and aides—with the exception of physical therapy assistants, who are better-paid.

Home health aides and personal care aides are "frequent flyers" on other good jobs list because they are expected to add so many jobs. There is no evidence, however, that they lead to better, higher-paying occupations within or out of health, and they are uniformly low-paying for all race/ ethnic groups. Although it is a potential first job or occupation for many, it is not a goal occupation.

Protective Service Occupations

The protective service occupations (Table A.8) do not require more than a high school diploma but do entail a significant amount of personal risk. Given that many are in local government, the occupations themselves are

TABLE A.7

Health Occupations

Occupation	Easy to Get	Grew 2010–2018	Projected 2018–2028	All Workers	Black Men	Black Women	Hispanic Men	Hispanic Women	White Men	White Women	Other Men	Other Women	OJT
Radiation therapist	Y	Y	Y	Y	Y	Y	Y	Y	Y	Y	Y	Y	
Respiratory therapist	Y	N	Y	Y	Y	Y	Y	Y	Y	Y	Y	Y	
Clinical laboratory technologist and technician		Y	Y	Y	Y	Y	Y	Y	Y	Y	Y	Y	
Dental hygienist	Y	Y	Y	Y	Y	Y	Y	Y	Y	Y	Y	Y	
Diagnostic-related technologist and technician	N	Y	Y	Y	Y	Y	Y	Y	Y	Y	Y	Y	
Emergency medical technician and paramedic	Y	Y	Y	Y	Y	Y	Y	Y	N	N	Y	Y	
Health diagnosing and treating practitioner support technician	N	Y	Y	N	Y	Y	Y	Y	N	N	Y	Y	L/M
Licensed Practical and Licensed Vocational Nurse	Y	Y	Y	Y	Y	Y	Y	Y	N	Y	Y	Y	
Medical records and health information technician	Y	N	Y	Y	Y	Y	Y	Y	Y	Y	Y	Y	
Optician, dispensing	Y	Y	Y	Y	Y	Y	Y	Y	Y	N	Y	Y	H
Health technologist and technician, not elsewhere classified	Y	Y	Y	Y	Y	Y	Y	Y	Y	Y	Y	Y	M

Table A.7—Continued

Occupation	Easy to Get	Grew 2010–2018	Projected 2018–2028	All Workers	Black Men	Black Women	Hispanic Men	Hispanic Women	White Men	White Women	Other Men	Other Women	OJT
Nursing, psychiatric, and home health aide	Y	Y	Y	N	N	N	N	N	N	N	N	N	L
Occupational therapy assistant and aide	Y	Y	Y	Y	Y	Y	Y	Y	Y	Y	Y	Y	L
Physical therapist assistant and aide	Y	Y	Y	N	Y	Y	Y	Y	Y	N	Y	Y	L
Massage therapists	Y	N	Y	N	Y	Y	Y	N	N	Y	N	Y	
Dental assistants	Y	N	Y	N	Y	N	Y	N	Y	N	Y	Y	
Medical assistant and other health care support occupations, not elsewhere classified	Y	Y	Y	N	N	N	N	N	N	N	N	Y	L/M

NOTES: 2010–2018 growth data and high-paying calculations derived from the CPS. Projected growth and rating of the amount of OJT is from the BLS EP. Y = yes; N = no. OJT options are none (blank), low ("L"), moderate ("M"), and high ("H"). High-paying is calculated as being above the median wage for subbaccalaureate workers, both overall ("All") and by race/ethnic-gender interaction. *Easy to get* is an indicator for an occupation not requiring prior experience—it is a true entry-level occupation.

not fast-growing or high-paying, but we tend to think of them as being stable and having good benefits, as well as being available outside of metropolitan areas. For this occupational family, we do not recommend any supervisor positions, since they require prior experience. In these occupations, we also discount earnings measures because public jobs are much more likely to have employer-sponsored health insurance and retirement benefits. Eliminating supervisor positions, we have police officer and detective, firefighter, fire inspector, and animal control that are added to the goal occupations. It could be the case that a security guard job is a good bridge to a police department, but this is very low-paying as a first job, and without

TABLE A.8
Protective Services Occupations

Occupation	Easy to Get	Grew 2010–2018	Projected 2018–2028	All Workers	Black Men	Black Women	Hispanic Men	Hispanic Women	White Men	White Women	Other Men	Other Women	OUT
First-line supervisor of correctional officers	N	N	N	Y	Y	N	Y	Y	Y	Y	Y	Y	
First-line supervisor of police and detectives	N	N	Y	Y	Y	Y	Y	Y	Y	Y	Y	Y	M
First-line supervisor of fire fighting and prevention workers	N	Y	Y	Y	Y	Y	Y	Y	Y	Y	Y	Y	M
Supervisor, protective service worker, all other	N	Y	Y	Y	Y	Y	Y	Y	N	Y	N	Y	
Firefighter	Y	N	Y	Y	Y	Y	Y	Y	Y	Y	Y	Y	H
Fire Inspector	N	N	Y	Y	Y	Y	Y	Y	Y	Y	Y	Y	M
Sheriff, bailiff, correctional officer, and jailer	Y	N	N	N	Y	N	Y	Y	N	N	Y	Y	M
Police officer and detectives	N	N	Y	Y	Y	N	Y	Y	Y	Y	Y	Y	M
Animal control	Y	Y	Y	N	Y	Y	Y	Y	N	N	Y	Y	M
Private detective and investigators	N	Y	Y	Y	Y	Y	N	Y	Y	Y	Y	Y	M

Table A.8—Continued

Occupation	Easy to Get	Grew 2010-2018	Projected 2018-2028	All Workers	Black Men	Black Women	Hispanic Men	Hispanic Women	White Men	White Women	Other Men	Other Women	OJT
Security guard and gaming surveillance officer	N	Y	Y	N	N	N	N	N	N	N	N	N	L/M
Crossing guard	Y	Y	Y	N	N	Y	Y	Y	N	N	N	Y	L
Law enforcement worker, not elsewhere classified	Y	Y	Y	N	N	N	N	N	N	N	Y	N	L/M

NOTES: 2010–2018 growth data and high-paying calculations derived from the CPS. Projected growth and rating of the amount of OJT is from the BLS EP. Y = yes; N = no. OJT options are none (blank), low ("L"), moderate ("M"), and high ("H"). High-paying is calculated as being above the median wage for subbaccalaureate workers, both overall ("All") and by race/ethnic-gender interaction. *Easy to get* is an indicator for an occupation not requiring prior experience—it is a true entry-level occupation.

a thorough analysis of the pathway viability, we cannot classify it as a goal occupation.

Food Preparation and Serving Occupations

Food preparation and serving (Table A.9) is a low-paying set of occupations, none of which require more than a high school diploma—if that is required. Although there are some instances in which bartenders, wait staff, and other workers at high-end, elite restaurants earn high salaries, this does not describe the majority of food preparation and service workers. In general, these are very low-paying jobs, often at the minimum wage. We do not add them to our list of goal occupations because we would not consider them aspirational occupations.

However, this does not mean that individuals should *never* acquire a job in food preparation and service occupations—indeed, they require no experience and are growing in the economy, so they should be some of the easier jobs to attain. The role that many food service jobs serve for an individual is as a first job that demonstrates basic workplace skills: getting in on time, following directions, working on a team. In that sense, they are a good job

TABLE A.9

Food Preparation and Service Occupations

Occupation	Easy to Get	Grew 2010–2018	Projected 2018–2028	All Workers	Black Men	Black Women	Hispanic Men	Hispanic Women	White Men	White Women	Other Men	Other Women	OJT
Chef and cook	N	Y	Y	N	N	N	N	N	N	N	N	N	L/M
First-line supervisor of food preparation and serving workers	N	N	Y	N	N	N	N	N	N	N	N	Y	
Food preparation worker	Y	Y	Y	N	N	N	N	N	N	N	N	N	L
Bartender	Y	Y	Y	N	N	N	N	N	N	N	N	N	L
Combined food preparation and serving worker, including fast food	Y	Y	Y	N	N	N	N	N	N	N	N	N	L
Counter attendant, cafeteria, food concession, and coffee shop	Y	N	Y	N	N	N	N	N	N	N	N	N	L
Waiter and waitress	Y	Y	Y	N	N	N	N	N	N	N	N	N	L
Food server, nonrestaurant	Y	Y	Y	N	N	N	N	N	N	N	N	N	L
Food preparation and serving-related worker, not elsewhere classified	Y	N	Y	N	N	N	N	N	N	N	N	N	L

Table A.9—Continued

Occupation	Easy to Get	Grew 2010–2018	Projected 2018–2028	All Workers	Black Men	Black Women	Hispanic Men	Hispanic Women	White Men	White Women	Other Men	Other Women	OJT
Dishwasher	Y	Y	Y	N	N	N	N	N	N	N	N	N	L
Host and hostess, restaurant, lounge, and coffee shop	Y	Y	Y	N	N	N	Y	N	N	N	N	N	L

NOTES: 2010–2018 growth data and high-paying calculations derived from the CPS. Projected growth and rating of the amount of OJT is from the BLS EP. Y = yes; N = no. OJT options are none (blank), low ("L"), moderate ("M"), and high ("H"). High-paying is calculated as being above the median wage for subbaccalaureate workers, both overall ("All") and by race/ethnic-gender interaction. *Easy to get* is an indicator for an occupation not requiring prior experience—it is a true entry-level occupation.

or good job placement for ChalleNGe, but this is not a reason to prioritize their skills in training.

Building and Grounds Cleaning and Maintenance Occupations

Cleaning occupations (Table A.10) are generally low-paying and not a bridge to better jobs after obtaining OJT. Some workers in these occupations are paid under the table, and they are generally thought to have a higher share of undocumented immigrants (e.g., Passel, 2006). As with food preparation and service occupations, we do not classify these as good occupations. Again, they could be a good initial placement, one that demonstrates work ethic and basic job skills, but not one that we would think of as needing investment or training.

Personal Care Occupations

Personal care and service (Table A.11) cover a set of occupations that are expected to grow considerably in the next ten years. The personal care aide is somewhat of an analogue to a home health aide. Unlike health aides and health occupations more generally, the personal care occupations are not

TABLE A.10

Building and Grounds Cleaning and Maintenance Occupations

Occupation	Easy to Get	Grew 2010–2018	Projected 2018–2028	All Workers	Black Men	Black Women	Hispanic Men	Hispanic Women	White Men	White Women	Other Men	Other Women	OJT
First-line supervisor of housekeeping and janitorial workers	N	N	Y	N	N	N	Y	Y	N	N	N	N	
First-line supervisor of landscaping, lawn service, and groundskeeping workers	N	N	Y	N	N	Y	N	Y	N	Y	Y	Y	
Janitor and building cleaner	Y	Y	Y	N	N	N	N	N	N	N	N	N	L
Maid and housekeeping cleaner	Y	Y	N	N	N	N	N	N	N	N	N	N	L
Pest control worker	Y	Y	Y	N	N	Y	N	Y	N	N	N	Y	M
Grounds maintenance worker	Y	Y	Y	N	N	Y	N	N	N	N	N	N	L/M

NOTES: 2010–2018 growth data and high-paying calculations derived from the CPS. Projected growth and rating of the amount of OJT is from the BLS EP. Y = yes; N = no. OJT options are none (blank), low ("L"), moderate ("M"), and high ("H"). High-paying is calculated as being above the median wage for subbaccalaureate workers, both overall ("All") and by race/ethnic-gender interaction. Easy to get is an indicator for an occupation not requiring prior experience—it is a true entry-level occupation.

split between a share that are high-paying and a share that are low-paying, or a share with high education and a share with low education; these occupations are generally lower-education and low-paying. While some (e.g., cosmetologist or barber) require subbaccalaureate training and thus could be classified as middle-skills jobs, the training cost generally dwarfs the potential earnings payoff. Finally, while tour and travel guide is an accessible, growing occupation with on-the-job training, it is regionally specific, and thus we cannot recommend pursuing it to a generalized population.

Sales Occupations

The outlook for sales occupations (Table A.12) is generally not good; many in-person sales jobs will be consolidated and replaced by online sales. Similar to food, cleaning, and personal care, many sales occupations are entry-level jobs with low pay, such as a cashier. There are a few exceptions to this. Sales representative for wholesale and manufacturing does not require prior experience and pays well. However, it is on the upper end of educational attainment among the subbaccalaureate occupations, with many (two- or four-year) college-educated workers. For this reason, we did not include it on our goal occupations.

Office and Administrative Support Occupations

Office and administrative support (Table A.13) spans 56 occupations, the vast majority of which are subbaccalaureate. These positions can be thought of as analogues to "technician" occupations that accompany many STEM occupations, but instead they support managers, business operations specialists, and finance specialists. In general, these occupations may have similarly low education requirements to many subbaccalaureate jobs but are in a more desirable setting and are considered "white collar" rather than "blue collar" occupations. Working for or next to highly paid office workers may also help lift wages and employer-provided benefits for support workers. However, many of these jobs are vulnerable to technological replacement or have been reduced due to technological developments in the past ten years (e.g., reductions in clerks and assistants due to software improvements that require fewer direct human inputs). Although the occupations in this family are not expected to grow overall, many specialized clerk positions have good employment prospects—and nearly all of these are associated with a high amount of OJT. Hence, we bundle most of the clerk positions in the *goal occupations* category.

TABLE A.11
Personal Care Occupations

Occupation	Easy to Get	Grew 2010–2018	Projected 2018–2028	All Workers	Black Men	Black Women	Hispanic Men	Hispanic Women	White Men	White Women	Other Men	Other Women	OJT
First-line supervisor of gaming workers	N	N	Y	N	Y	N	Y	Y	Y	N	Y	Y	
First-line supervisor of personal service workers	N	N	Y	N	N	Y	N	Y	N	N	N	N	
Animal trainer	Y	N	Y	N	Y	Y	Y	Y	Y	N	Y	Y	M
Nonfarm animal caretaker	Y	Y	Y	N	N	N	N	N	N	N	Y	N	L
Gaming services worker	Y	N	Y	N	N	Y	Y	N	N	N	N	N	L
Usher, lobby attendant, and ticket taker[a]	Y	N	Y	N									L
Entertainment attendant and related worker, not elsewhere classified	Y	N	Y	N	N	N	N	N	N	N	N	N	L
Funeral service worker and embalmer	Y	Y	Y	Y	N	Y	Y	Y	N	Y	Y	Y	L/M
Barber	Y	N	Y	N	N	Y	N	Y	Y	N	N	Y	
Hairdresser, hairstylist, and cosmetologist	Y	Y	Y	N	Y	N	N	N	N	N	N	N	

Table A.11—Continued

Occupation	Easy to Get	Grew 2010–2018	Projected 2018–2028	All Workers	Black Men	Black Women	Hispanic Men	Hispanic Women	White Men	White Women	Other Men	Other Women	OJT
Personal appearance worker, not elsewhere classified	Y	Y	Y	N	N	N	Y	N	Y	N	N	N	L
Baggage porter, bellhop, and concierge	Y	Y	Y	N	N	N	Y	Y	N	N	N	Y	L/M
Tour and travel guide	Y	Y	Y	N	Y	Y	Y	Y	N	N	Y	Y	M
Child care worker	Y	Y	Y	N	Y	N	N	N	N	N	Y	N	L
Personal care aide	Y	Y	Y	N	N	N	N	N	N	N	N	N	L
Recreation and fitness worker	Y	N	Y	N	N	N	N	Y	N	N	Y	Y	L
Residential advisor	Y	N	Y	N	N	N	N	N	N	N	Y	Y	L
Personal care and service workers, all other	Y	Y	Y	N	N	N	N	N	N	N	N	N	L

NOTES: 2010–2018 growth data and high-paying calculations derived from the CPS. Projected growth and rating of the amount of OJT is from the BLS EP. Y = yes; N = no. OJT options are ncne (blank), low ("L"), moderate ("M"), and high ("H"). High-paying is calculated as being above the median wage for subbaccalaureate workers, both overall ("All") and by race/ethnic-gender interaction. BM = Black male; BF = Black female; HM = Hispanic male; HF = Hispanic female; WM = White male; WF = White female; OM = Other male; and OF = Other female. Easy to get is an indicator for an occupation not requiring prior experience—it is a true entry-level occupation.

a Sample was too small to perform subgroup wage analysis.

TABLE A.12
Sales Occupations

Occupation	Easy to Get	Grew 2010–2018	Projected 2018–2028	All Workers	Black Men	Black Women	Hispanic Men	Hispanic Women	White Men	White Women	Other Men	Other Women	OJT
First-line supervisor of sales workers	N	Y	N	N	Y	N	Y	Y	N	N	N	N	
Cashier	Y	Y	N	N	N	N	N	N	N	N	N	N	L
Counter and rental clerk	Y	N	Y	N	N	N	N	N	N	N	N	N	L
Parts salesperson	Y	N	N	N	N	Y	N	N	N	Y	N	Y	M
Retail salesperson	Y	Y	N	N	N	N	N	N	N	N	N	N	L
Advertising sales agent	Y	Y	Y	N	Y	Y	Y	Y	Y	Y	Y	Y	M
Insurance sales agent	Y	Y	N	N	Y	Y	Y	Y	N	Y	N	Y	M
Travel agent	Y	N	N	N	N	Y	Y	Y	Y	Y	Y	Y	M
Sales representative, services, all other	Y	N	Y	Y	N	N	Y	N	Y	Y	Y	N	M

Table A.12—Continued

Occupation	Easy to Get	Grew 2010–2018	Projected 2018–2028	All Workers	Black Men	Black Women	Hispanic Men	Hispanic Women	White Men	White Women	Other Men	Other Women	OJT
Sales representative, wholesale and manufacturing	Y	Y	Y	Y	Y	Y	Y	Y	Y	Y	N	Y	M
Model, demonstrator, and product promoter	Y	N	Y	N	Y	N	Y	Y	N	N	Y	Y	L
Real estate broker and sales agent	N	Y	Y	N	N	N	Y	Y	Y	Y	Y	N	M
Telemarketer	Y	N	N	N	Y	N	N	N	N	N	N	Y	L
Door-to-door sales worker, news and street vendor, and related worker	Y	Y		N	N	Y	Y	Y	N	N	Y	Y	L
Sales and related worker, all other	Y	Y	Y	N	Y	N	Y	N	N	N	Y	N	

NOTES: 2010–2018 growth data and high-paying calculations derived from the CPS. Projected growth and rating of the amount of OJT is from the BLS EP. Y = yes; N = no. OJT options are none (blank), low ("L"), moderate ("M"), and high ("H"). High-paying is calculated as being above the median wage for subbaccalaureate workers, both overall ("All") and by race/ethnic-gender interaction. *Easy to get* is an indicator for an occupation not requiring prior experience—it is a true entry-level occupation.

TABLE A.13

Office and Administrative Support Occupations

Occupation	Easy to Get	Grew 2010–2018	Projected 2018–2028	All Workers	Black Men	Black Women	Hispanic Men	Hispanic Women	White Men	White Women	Other Men	Other Women	OJT
Bookkeeping, accounting, and auditing clerk	Y	N	N	N	N	Y	N	Y	N	Y	Y	Y	M
New account clerk	Y	N	N	N	Y	Y	Y	N	Y	N	Y	Y	M
Correspondent clerk and order clerk	Y	N	N	N	Y	Y	N	N	N	N	Y	Y	L
Human resources assistant, except payroll and timekeeping	Y	N	N	Y	Y	N	Y	Y	N	Y	Y	Y	
Office and administrative support worker, not elsewhere classified	Y	Y	Y	N	Y	Y	Y	Y	N	Y	Y	Y	L
Communications equipment operator, all other	Y	Y	Y	N	Y	Y	Y	Y	Y	Y	Y	Y	L
Billing and posting clerk	Y	N	Y	N	N	Y	N	Y	N	Y	N	Y	M
Gaming cage worker	Y	Y	Y	N	Y	Y	Y	Y	Y	N	N	N	L
Financial clerk, not elsewhere classified	Y	N	Y	N	Y	Y	Y	Y	Y	Y	Y	Y	L

Table A.13—Continued

Occupation	Easy to Get	Grew 2010–2018	Projected 2018–2028	All Workers	Black Men	Black Women	Hispanic Men	Hispanic Women	White Men	White Women	Other Men	Other Women	OJT
Brokerage clerk	Y	Y	Y	Y	Y	Y	Y	Y	Y	Y	Y	Y	M
Court, municipal, and license clerk	Y	N	Y	Y	Y	Y	Y	Y	Y	Y	Y	Y	H
Eligibility interviewer, government programs	Y	N	Y	Y	Y	Y	Y	Y	Y	Y	Y	Y	M
Interviewer, except eligibility and loan	Y	N	Y	N	Y	N	N	Y	N	N	Y	N	L
Loan interviewer and clerk	Y	N	Y	Y	Y	Y	Y	Y	N	Y	Y	Y	L
Receptionist and information clerk	Y	N	Y	N	N	Y	N	N	N	N	N	N	L
Reservation and transportation ticket agent and travel clerk	Y	Y	Y	N	Y	Y	N	Y	Y	N	Y	Y	L
Information and record clerk, all other	Y	Y	Y	N	Y	Y	Y	Y	N	N	Y	Y	L
Cargo and freight agent	Y	Y	Y	Y	Y	Y	Y	Y	Y	Y	Y	Y	L
Courier and messenger	Y	N	Y	N	N	Y	N	Y	N	Y	Y	Y	L

Table A.13—Continued

Occupation	Easy to Get	Grew 2010–2018	Projected 2018–2028	All Workers	Black Men	Black Women	Hispanic Men	Hispanic Women	White Men	White Women	Other Men	Other Women	OJT
Dispatcher	Y	N	Y	N	Y	Y	Y	Y	N	N	Y	Y	M
Production, planning, and expediting clerk	Y	N	Y	Y	Y	Y	Y	Y	Y	Y	Y	Y	M
Insurance claims and policy processing clerk	Y	N	Y	N	N	Y	N	Y	N	Y	Y	Y	M
First-line supervisor of office and administrative support workers	N	N	N	Y	Y	Y	Y	Y	N	Y	Y	Y	
Switchboard operator, including answering service	Y	N	N	N	Y	N	Y	Y	N	Y	Y	Y	L
Telephone operator	Y	N	N	N	Y	N	Y	N	N	Y	Y	Y	L
Bill and account collector	Y	N	N	N	N	Y	Y	Y	N	N	Y	N	M
Payroll and timekeeping clerk	Y	N	N	Y	Y	Y	Y	Y	Y	Y	Y	Y	M
Procurement clerk	Y	N	N	Y	Y	Y	Y	Y	Y	Y	Y	Y	M
Bank teller	Y	N	N	N	Y	N	N	N	N	N	Y	Y	L

Table A.13—Continued

Occupation	Easy to Get	Grew 2010–2018	Projected 2018–2028	All Workers	Black Men	Black Women	Hispanic Men	Hispanic Women	White Men	White Women	Other Men	Other Women	OJT
Credit authorizer, checker, and clerk	Y	N	N	N	Y	N	N	Y	Y	Y	Y	Y	M
Customer service representative	Y	Y	N	N	N	Y	N	N	N	N	N	N	L
File clerk	Y	N	N	N	Y	Y	N	Y	Y	Y	Y	Y	L
Hotel, motel, and resort desk clerk	Y	Y	N	N	N	N	N	N	N	N	N	N	L
Library assistant, clerical	Y	N	N	N	Y	Y	Y	Y	Y	N	Y	Y	L
Meter reader, utilities	Y	N	N	N	N	Y	Y	Y	Y	Y	Y	Y	L
Postal Service clerks	Y	Y	N	Y	N	Y	Y	Y	Y	Y	Y	Y	L
Postal Service mail carrier	Y	N	N	Y	Y	Y	Y	Y	Y	Y	Y	Y	L
Postal Service mail sorter, processor, and processing machine operator	Y	N	N	Y	N	Y	N	Y	Y	Y	Y	Y	L
Shipping, receiving, and traffic clerk	Y	N	N	N	N	N	N	N	N	N	N	N	L
Stock clerk and order filler	Y	Y	Y	N	N	N	N	N	N	N	N	N	L

126

Table A.13—Continued

Occupation	Easy to Get	Grew 2010–2018	Projected 2018–2028	All Workers	Black Men	Black Women	Hispanic Men	Hispanic Women	White Men	White Women	Other Men	Other Women	OJT
Weigher, measurer, checker, and sampler, recordkeeping	Y	N	Y	N	N	Y	N	Y	N	N	N	Y	L
Secretary and administrative assistant	N	N	N	N	Y	Y	Y	Y	N	Y	Y	Y	L/M
Computer operator	Y	Y	N	Y	Y	Y	Y	Y	Y	N	Y	Y	M
Data entry keyer	Y	N	N	N	Y	Y	N	Y	N	N	Y	Y	L
Word processor and typist	Y	N	N	Y	Y	Y	Y	Y	N	Y	Y	Y	L
Mail clerk and mail machine operator, except Postal Service	Y	N	N	N	N	Y	N	Y	N	Y	Y	Y	L
Office clerk, general	Y	Y	N	N	Y	N	N	Y	N	N	N	Y	L
Office machine operator, except computer	Y	N	N	N	Y	Y	Y	Y	N	Y	Y	Y	L

NOTES: 2010–2018 growth data and high-paying calculations derived from the CPS. Projected growth and rating of the amount of OJT is from the BLS EP. Y = yes; N = no. OJT options are none (blank), low ("L"), moderate ("M"), and high ("H"). High-paying is calculated as being above the median wage for subbaccalaureate workers, both overall ("All") and by race/ethnic-gender interaction. *Easy to get* is an indicator for an occupation not requiring prior experience—it is a true entry-level occupation.

Construction Occupations

Construction occupations (Table A.14) support the construction of buildings, roads, and other structures. In some ways, they are the "support" occupations for architects and engineers. Construction occupations are high-paying, many are unionized, and, in general, are thought to be growing. Although there was a sharp downturn among construction workers after the housing bubble burst, it is now thought that with the need for infrastructure upgrades, these will remain in steady demand. Construction sites are also helpful for workers wanting to learn an occupation, as many specialists and tradespeople work in tandem. Many sites rely on low-paid workers with little experience who can then "survey" the occupations and if inclined, invest in one occupation. This confluence of more and less experienced workers on a team, especially under the apprenticeship model, allows new occupation entrants to learn from experienced mentors.

In this occupation family, all the occupations are expected to grow in the next ten years, and all but two do not require prior experience; most also have a significant amount of OJT. Most of the occupations pay above the median, and if they do not, they pay above the median for some groups. We recommend the majority for the goal occupations list. Note that the "construction worker, not elsewhere classified" category includes solar photovoltaic installers, which is frequently cited in the press as a high-paying, quickly growing occupation. However, as with other energy occupations, employment in this occupation is generally fairly region-specific (explored further in Appendix B).

Extraction Occupations

Extraction occupations (Table A.15) are comparable with the construction occupations in that they are hands-on, physical labor in growth industries and associated with high pay and training. We did not add these to the goal occupations list because, while the skills will generally overlap with construction and installation, the occupations are geographically concentrated. To the extent that the skills are similar to those involved in construction, the O*NET will capture these elements.

TABLE A.14
Construction Occupations

Occupation	Easy to Get	Grew 2010–2018	Projected 2018–2028	All Workers	Black Men	Black Women	Hispanic Men	Hispanic Women	White Men	White Women	Other Men	Other Women	OJT
First-Line supervisor of construction trades and extraction workers	N	N	Y	Y	Y	Y	Y	Y	Y	Y	Y	Y	
Boilermaker	Y	N	Y	Y	Y	Y	Y	Y	Y	Y	Y	Y	
Brickmason, blockmason, and stonemason	Y	Y	Y	Y	Y	Y	N	Y	Y	Y	Y	Y	
Carpenter	Y	Y	Y	Y	Y	Y	N	Y	Y	N	Y	Y	
Carpet, floor, and tile installer and finisher	Y	Y	Y	N	Y	Y	N	Y	N	Y	Y	Y	L/M/H
Cement mason, concrete finisher, and terrazzo worker	Y	N	Y	Y	N	Y	Y	Y	Y	Y	Y	Y	M
Construction laborer	Y	Y	Y	N	N	Y	N	Y	N	N	N	Y	L
Paving, surfacing, and tamping equipment operator	Y	N	Y	Y	Y	Y	Y	Y	N	Y	Y	Y	M

Table A.14—Continued

Occupation	Easy to Get	Grew 2010–2018	Projected 2018–2028	All Workers	Black Men	Black Women	Hispanic Men	Hispanic Women	White Men	White Women	Other Men	Other Women	OJT
Construction equipment operator except paving, surfacing, and tamping equipment operator	Y	N	Y	Y	Y	Y	Y	Y	Y	Y	Y	Y	M
Drywall installer, ceiling tile installer, and taper	Y	Y	Y	N	N	Y	N	Y	N	Y	Y	Y	M
Electrician	Y	Y	Y	Y	Y	N	Y	N	Y	Y	Y	Y	
Glazier	Y	N	Y	Y	Y	Y	Y	Y	Y	Y	N	Y	
Insulation worker	Y	Y	Y	Y	Y	Y	Y	Y	Y	Y	Y	Y	L
Painter, construction and maintenance	Y	Y	Y	N	N	Y	N	N	Y	N	N	Y	M/H
Paperhanger[a,b]		N	Y	N									
Pipelayer, plumber, pipefitter, and steamfitter	Y	Y	Y	Y	Y	Y	Y	Y	Y	Y	Y	Y	L
Plasterer and stucco mason	Y	N	Y	N	Y	Y	N	Y	N	Y	Y	Y	H

Table A.14—Continued

Occupation	Easy to Get	Grew 2010–2018	Projected 2018–2028	All Workers	Black Men	Black Women	Hispanic Men	Hispanic Women	White Men	White Women	Other Men	Other Women	OJT
Reinforcing iron and rebar worker[a]	Y	N	Y	N									
Roofer	Y	Y	Y	N	N	Y	N	Y	N	Y	Y	Y	M
Sheet metal worker, metal-working	Y	Y	Y	Y	Y	Y	Y	Y	Y	Y	Y	Y	
Structural iron and steel worker	Y	N	Y	Y	Y	Y	Y	Y	Y	Y	Y	Y	
Helper, construction trades	Y	Y	Y	N	N	Y	N	Y	N	Y	Y	Y	L
Construction and building inspector	N	N	Y	Y	Y	Y	Y	Y	Y	Y	Y	Y	M
Elevator installer and repairer	Y	N	Y	Y	Y	Y	Y	Y	Y	Y	Y	Y	
Fence erector	Y	N	Y	N	Y	Y	N	Y	N	Y	Y	Y	M
Hazardous materials removal worker	Y	N	Y	Y	Y	Y	Y	Y	Y	Y	Y	Y	M

Table A.14—Continued

Occupation	Easy to Get	Grew 2010–2018	Projected 2018–2028	All Workers	Black Men	Black Women	Hispanic Men	Hispanic Women	White Men	White Women	Other Men	Other Women	OJT
Highway maintenance worker	Y	Y	Y	Y	Y	Y	N	Y	Y	Y	Y	Y	M
Rail-track laying and maintenance equipment operator	Y	N	Y	Y	Y	Y	Y	Y	Y	Y	Y	Y	M
Construction worker, not elsewhere classified[c]	Y	Y	Y	Y	Y	Y	Y	Y	Y	Y	Y	Y	M

NOTES: 2010–2018 growth data and high-paying calculations derived from the CPS. Projected growth and rating of the amount of OJT is from the BLS EP. Y = yes; N = no. OJT options are none (blank), low ("L"), moderate ("M"), and high ("H"). High-paying is calculated as being above the median wage for subbaccalaureate workers, both overall ("All") and by race/ethnic-gender interaction. *Easy to get* is an indicator for an occupation not requiring prior experience—it is a true entry-level occupation.

[a] Sample was too small to perform subgroup wage analysis.

[b] Not all occupations were available for education analysis.

[c] Category includes solar photovoltaic installers. Data for solar photovoltaic installers alone is not available from the CPS (the code includes all unclassified construction workers).

Installation, Maintenance, and Repair Occupations

Installation, maintenance, and repair occupations (Table A.16) cover the installation, maintenance, and repair of equipment. There are many parallels with construction occupations. Some construction workers are essentially installation and repair workers that specialize in buildings and roads; installation and repair occupations cover everything else—from planes to cell towers. These occupations are physical and expected to grow in the next ten years and pay above the median. Similar to construction, these occupations are both growing and high-paying. Consequently, we recommend many for the goal occupations list.

TABLE A.15

Extraction Occupations

Occupation	Easy to Get	Grew 2010–2018	Projected 2018–2028	All Workers	Black Men	Black Women	Hispanic Men	Hispanic Women	White Men	White Women	Other Men	Other Women	OJT
Derrick, rotary drill, and service unit operator, and roustabout, oil, gas, and mining	Y	Y	Y	Y	Y	Y	Y	Y	Y	Y	Y	Y	L/M
Earth driller, except oil and gas	Y	Y	Y	Y	Y	Y	Y	Y	Y	Y	Y	Y	M
Explosives worker, ordnance handling expert, and blaster	N	Y	Y	Y	Y	Y	Y	Y	Y	Y	Y	Y	H
Mining machine operator	Y	N	Y	Y	Y	Y	Y	Y	Y	Y	Y	Y	M
Extraction worker, not elsewhere classified	Y	N	Y	Y	Y	Y	Y	Y	Y	Y	Y	Y	L/M

NOTES: 2010–2018 growth data and high-paying calculations derived from the CPS. Projected growth and rating of the amount of OJT is from the BLS EP. Y = yes; N = no. OJT options are none (blank), low ("L"), moderate ("M"), and high ("H"). High-paying is calculated as being above the median wage for subbaccalaureate workers, both overall ("All") and by race/ethnic-gender interaction. *Easy to get* is an indicator for an occupation not requiring prior experience—it is a true entry-level occupation.

Production Occupations

Production occupations (Table A.17) span 71 different specific occupations, none of which requires a baccalaureate degree. Production workers work in the manufacturing industry, for the most part. Although these occupations are historically associated with high unionization rates, good wages, and nonwage benefits, the demand for these workers has fallen over time—and will continue to fall, as much of the production process becomes computerized. However, that does not mean that there are no production jobs or careers. We do not recommend any production occupations, similar to extraction occupations, because jobs in these occupations are not broadly distributed geographically. In addition, production jobs will likely develop around employer-specific skill needs. Hence, workers interested in production should find a local employer with a secure opportunity; we would not recommend this occupation's skills for a more generally focused training program.

Transportation and Material Moving Occupations

Transportation and material moving workers (Table A.18) support the movement of people and objects from place to place in the air, on the water, on the track, and on the road. These jobs do not have the same level of computerization threat that production occupations do. While autonomous vehicles are likely to supplant some employment among these occupations, the high rate of unionization and technical skills required for many of them make the occupation family less likely to see substantial employment shifts (*Stick Shift: Autonomous Vehicles, Driving Jobs, and the Future of Work*, 2017). A subset of these occupations is growing and projected to continue to grow; we recommend several that also include substantial OJT.

TABLE A.16
Installation, Maintenance, and Repair Occupations

Occupation	Easy to Get	Grew 2010–2018	Projected 2018–2028	All Workers	Black Men	Black Women	Hispanic Men	Hispanic Women	White Men	White Women	Other Men	Other Women	OJT
First-line supervisor of mechanics, installers, and repairers	N	N	Y	Y	Y	Y	Y	Y	Y	Y	Y	Y	
Computer, automated teller, and office machine repairer	Y	N	N	Y	Y	Y	Y	Y	Y	Y	Y	Y	L
Radio and telecommunications equipment installer and repairer	Y	N	N	Y	Y	Y	Y	Y	Y	Y	Y	Y	M
Avionics technician	Y	Y	Y	Y	Y	Y	Y	Y	Y	Y	Y	Y	
Electric motor, power tool, and related repairer	N	Y	Y	Y	Y	Y	Y	Y	Y	Y	Y	Y	M
Electrical and electronics repairer, transportation equipment, and industrial and utility	N	N	Y	Y	Y	Y	Y	Y	Y	Y	Y	Y	M/H

Table A.16—Continued

Occupation	Easy to Get	Grew 2010–2018	Projected 2018–2028	All Workers	Black Men	Black Women	Hispanic Men	Hispanic Women	White Men	White Women	Other Men	Other Women	OJT
Electronic equipment installer and repairer, motor vehicles	Y	N	N	Y	Y	Y	Y	Y	Y	Y	Y	Y	M
Electronic home entertainment equipment installer and repairer	Y	N	N	Y	Y	Y	Y	Y	Y	Y	Y	Y	L
Security and fire alarm systems installer	Y	N	Y	Y	Y	Y	Y	Y	Y	Y	Y	Y	M
Aircraft mechanic and service technician	Y	Y	Y	Y	Y	Y	Y	Y	Y	Y	Y	Y	
Automotive body and related repairer	Y	N	Y	Y	N	Y	N	Y	Y	N	Y	Y	H
Automotive glass installers and repairer	Y	Y	Y	Y	Y	Y	N	Y	Y	Y	Y	Y	M
Automotive service technician and mechanic	Y	Y	N	Y	Y	Y	N	Y	N	Y	Y	Y	L

Table A.16—Continued

Occupation	Easy to Get	Grew 2010–2018	Projected 2018–2028	All Workers	Black Men	Black Women	Hispanic Men	Hispanic Women	White Men	White Women	Other Men	Other Women	OJT
Bus and truck mechanic and diesel engine specialist	Y	Y	Y	Y	Y	Y	Y	Y	Y	Y	Y	Y	M
Heavy vehicle and mobile equipment service technician and mechanic	Y	N	Y	Y	Y	Y	Y	Y	Y	Y	Y	Y	M
Small engine mechanic	Y	N	Y	Y	Y	Y	Y	Y	N	Y	Y	Y	L/M/H
Vehicle and mobile equipment mechanic, installer, and repairer, not elsewhere classified	Y	N	N	N	Y	Y	N	Y	N	Y	N	Y	L/M/H
Control and valve installer and repairer	Y		Y	Y	Y	Y	Y	Y	Y	Y	Y	Y	M
Heating, air conditioning, and refrigeration mechanic and installer	Y	Y		Y	Y	Y	Y	Y	Y	Y	Y	Y	H
Home appliance repairer	Y	Y	N	Y	Y	Y	Y	Y	Y	Y	Y	Y	M

Table A.16—Continued

Occupation	Easy to Get	Grew 2010–2018	Projected 2018–2028	All Workers	Black Men	Black Women	Hispanic Men	Hispanic Women	White Men	White Women	Other Men	Other Women	OJT
Industrial and refractory machinery mechanic	Y	N	Y	Y	Y	Y	Y	Y	Y	N	Y	Y	M/H
Maintenance and repair worker, general	Y	Y	Y	Y	Y	Y	Y	Y	Y	Y	Y	Y	M
Maintenance worker, machinery	Y	N	Y	Y	Y	Y	Y	Y	Y	Y	Y	Y	H
Millwright	Y	N	Y	Y	Y	Y	Y	Y	Y	Y	Y	Y	
Electrical power-line installer and repairer	Y	N	Y	Y	Y	Y	Y	Y	Y	Y	Y	Y	H
Telecommunications line installer and repairer	Y	Y	Y	Y	Y	Y	Y	Y	Y	Y	Y	Y	H
Precision instrument and equipment repairer	Y	Y	Y	Y	Y	Y	Y	Y	Y	N	Y	Y	M/H
Coin, vending, and amusement machine servicer and repairer	Y	N	Y	N	Y	Y	Y	Y	N	N	Y	Y	L

Table A.16—Continued

Occupation	Easy to Get	Grew 2010–2018	Projected 2018–2028	All Workers	Black Men	Black Women	Hispanic Men	Hispanic Women	White Men	White Women	Other Men	Other Women	OJT
Locksmith and safe repairer	Y	N	N	Y	Y	Y	Y	Y	Y	Y	Y	Y	H
Manufactured building and mobile home installer	Y	N	N	N	Y	Y	N	Y	N	Y	Y	Y	L
Rigger	Y	Y	Y	Y	Y	Y	Y	Y	Y	Y	Y	Y	M
Helper—installation, maintenance, and repair workers	Y	Y	Y	N	N	Y	N	Y	N	Y	Y	Y	L
Other installation, maintenance, and repair worker including wind turbine service technician, commercial diver, and signal and track switch repairer	Y	N	Y	Y	Y	Y	Y	N	Y	Y	Y	Y	M/H

NOTES: 2010–2018 growth data and high-paying calculations derived from the CPS. Projected growth and rating of the amount of OJT is from the BLS EP. Y = yes; N = no. OJT options are none (blank), low ("L"), moderate ("M"), and high ("H"). High-paying is calculated as being above the median wage for subbaccalaureate workers, both overall ("All") and by race/ethnic-gender interaction. *Easy to get* is an indicator for an occupation not requiring prior experience—it is a true entry-level occupation.

TABLE A.17
Production Occupations

Occupation	Easy to Get	Grew 2010–2018	Projected 2018–2028	All Workers	Black Men	Black Women	Hispanic Men	Hispanic Women	White Men	White Women	Other Men	Other Women	OJT
First-line supervisor of production and operating workers	N	Y	N	Y	Y	N	Y	Y	Y	Y	Y	Y	
Aircraft structure, surfaces, rigging, and systems assembler	Y	N	N	Y	Y	Y	Y	Y	Y	N	Y	Y	M
Electrical, electronics, and electromechanical assembler	Y	Y	N	N	N	N	N	N	N	N	Y	Y	M
Engine and other machine assembler	Y	N	N	N	Y	Y	Y	Y	N	Y	Y	Y	M
Structural metal fabricator and fitter	Y	Y	N	Y	Y	Y	Y	Y	Y	Y	N	Y	M
Assemblers and fabricators, not elsewhere classified	Y	Y	N	N	N	N	N	N	N	N	N	N	M
Baker	Y	N	Y	N	N	N	N	N	N	N	N	N	H

Table A.17—Continued

Occupation	Easy to Get	Grew 2010–2018	Projected 2018–2028	All Workers	Black Men	Black Women	Hispanic Men	Hispanic Women	White Men	White Women	Other Men	Other Women	OJT
Butcher and other meat, poultry, and fish processing worker	Y	N	Y	N	N	N	N	N	N	N	N	N	L/M
Food and tobacco roasting, baking, and drying machine operator and tender	Y	N	Y	N	Y	Y	Y	Y	N	Y	Y	Y	M
Food batchmaker	Y	N	Y	N	Y	N	N	N	N	N	Y	Y	M
Food cooking machine operator and tender	Y	Y	Y	N	Y	Y	N	Y	N	N	Y	Y	M
Food processing, not elsewhere classified	Y	N	Y	N	N	N	N	N	N	N	N	Y	M
Computer control programmer and operator	Y	Y	N	Y	Y	Y	Y	Y	Y	N	Y	Y	M
Extruding and drawing machine setter, operator, and tender, metal and plastic	Y	Y	N	N	Y	Y	Y	Y	N	N	Y	Y	M

Table A.17—Continued

Occupation	Easy to Get	Grew 2010–2018	Projected 2018–2028	All Workers	Black Men	Black Women	Hispanic Men	Hispanic Women	White Men	White Women	Other Men	Other Women	OJT
Forging machine setter, operator, and tender, metal and plastic[a]		N	Y	N	N								
Rolling machine setter, operator, and tender, metal and plastic	Y	N	N	N	N	Y	N	Y	N	Y	Y	Y	M
Cutting, punching, and press machine setter, operator, and tender, metal and plastic	Y	N	N	N	N	Y	N	N	N	N	N	N	M
Drilling and boring machine tool setter, operator, and tender, metal and plastic[a]		N	Y	N									
Grinding, lapping, polishing, and buffing machine tool setter, operator, and tender, metal and plastic	Y	N	N	N	Y	Y	Y	Y	N	Y	Y	Y	M

Table A.17—Continued

Occupation	Easy to Get	Grew 2010–2018	Projected 2018–2028	All Workers	Black Men	Black Women	Hispanic Men	Hispanic Women	White Men	White Women	Other Men	Other Women	OJT
Lathe and turning machine tool setter, operator, and tender, metal and plastic	Y	N	N	Y	Y	Y	Y	Y	N	Y	Y	Y	M
Machinist	Y	N	Y	Y	Y	Y	Y	Y	Y	Y	Y	Y	H
Metal furnace operator, tender, pourer, and caster	Y	Y	N	Y	Y	Y	Y	Y	N	Y	Y	Y	M
Model maker and patternmaker, metal and plastic[a]		N	Y	N									
Molder and molding machine setter, operator, and tender, metal and plastic	Y	Y	N	N	Y	Y	N	Y	N	N	Y	N	M
Tool and die maker	Y	Y	Y	Y	Y	Y	N	Y	Y	Y	Y	Y	H
Welding, soldering, and brazing worker	Y	Y	Y	Y	N	Y	Y	Y	N	Y	Y	Y	M

143

Table A.17—Continued

Occupation	Easy to Get	Grew 2010–2018	Projected 2018–2028	All Workers	Black Men	Black Women	Hispanic Men	Hispanic Women	White Men	White Women	Other Men	Other Women	OJT
Heat treating equipment setter, operator, and tender, metal and plastic[a]	Y	N	Y	N									
Plating and coating machine setter, operator, and tender, metal and plastic	Y	Y	N	N	Y	Y	Y	Y	N	Y	Y	Y	M
Tool grinder, filer, and sharpener	Y	N	N	Y	Y	Y	Y	Y	Y	Y	Y	Y	M
Metal worker and plastic worker, not elsewhere classified	Y	Y	N	N	N	N	N	N	N	N	Y	N	M
Bookbinder, printing machine operator, and job printer	Y	N	N	N	Y	Y	N	N	N	N	Y	Y	M
Prepress technician and worker	Y	N	N	Y	Y	Y	Y	Y	Y	N	Y	Y	
Laundry and dry-cleaning worker	Y	N	N	N	N	N	N	N	N	N	Y	N	L

Table A.17—Continued

Occupation	Easy to Get	Grew 2010–2018	Projected 2018–2028	All Workers	Black Men	Black Women	Hispanic Men	Hispanic Women	White Men	White Women	Other Men	Other Women	OJT
Textile winding, twisting, and drawing out machine setter, operator, and tender	Y	Y	N	N	Y	Y	Y	N	Y	Y	Y	Y	M
Upholsterer	Y	Y	N	N	Y	Y	N	Y	N	N	Y	Y	M
Textile, apparel, and furnishings worker, not elsewhere classified	Y	Y	N	N	N	N	N	N	N	Y	N	Y	L/M
Cabinetmaker and bench carpenter	Y	Y	N	N	Y	N	Y	N	N	N	N	Y	M
Furniture finisher	Y	Y	N	Y	Y	Y	Y	Y	N	Y	Y	Y	L
Sawing machine setter, operator, and tender, wood	Y	Y	N	N	N	N	N	Y	N	N	Y	Y	M
Woodworking machine setter, operator, and tender, except sawing	Y	Y	N	N	Y	Y	N	Y	N	N	Y	Y	M

Table A.17—Continued

Occupation	Easy to Get	Grew 2010–2018	Projected 2018–2028	All Workers	Black Men	Black Women	Hispanic Men	Hispanic Women	White Men	White Women	Other Men	Other Women	OJT
Presser, textile, garment, and related materials	Y	N	N	N	Y	N	N	N	N	N	Y	N	L
Sewing machine operator	Y	N	N	N	N	N	N	N	N	N	Y	N	L
Shoe and leather worker and repairer	Y	N	N	N	Y	Y	N	N	Y	Y	Y	Y	M
Shoe machine operator and tender[a]		N	Y	N									
Tailor, dressmaker, and sewer	Y	N	N	N	N	N	N	N	Y	N	Y	Y	M
Textile bleaching and dyeing, and cutting machine setter, operator, and tender	Y	Y	N	N	Y	Y	N	Y	N	Y	Y	Y	M
Textile knitting and weaving machine setter, operator, and tender	Y	N	N	N	Y	Y	Y	N	N	N	Y	Y	L

Table A.17—Continued

Occupation	Easy to Get	Grew 2010–2018	Projected 2018–2028	All Workers	Black Men	Black Women	Hispanic Men	Hispanic Women	White Men	White Women	Other Men	Other Women	OJT
Woodworker including model maker and patternmaker, not elsewhere classified	Y	N	Y	Y	Y	Y	Y	Y	N	Y	Y	Y	M
Power plant operator, distributor, and dispatcher	Y	N	N	Y	Y	Y	Y	Y	Y	Y	Y	Y	H
Stationary engineer and boiler operator	Y	N	Y	Y	Y	Y	Y	Y	Y	Y	Y	Y	H
Water treatment plant and system operator	Y	Y	N	Y	Y	Y	Y	Y	Y	Y	Y	Y	H
Plant and system operator, not elsewhere classified	Y	Y	N	Y	Y	Y	Y	Y	Y	Y	Y	Y	M/H
Chemical processing machine setter, operator, and tender	Y	Y	N	Y	Y	Y	Y	Y	Y	Y	Y	Y	M

Table A.17—Continued

Occupation	Easy to Get	Grew 2010–2018	Projected 2018–2028	All Workers	Black Men	Black Women	Hispanic Men	Hispanic Women	White Men	White Women	Other Men	Other Women	OJT
Crushing, grinding, polishing, mixing, and blending worker	Y	N	N	N	Y	Y	N	N	N	N	Y	Y	M
Cutting worker	Y	N	N	N	N	N	N	N	N	N	Y	Y	L/M
Extruding, forming, pressing, and compacting machine setter, operator, and tender	Y	N	N	N	Y	Y	N	Y	N	N	Y	Y	M
Furnace, kiln, oven, drier, and kettle operator and tender	Y	N	N	N	Y	Y	N	Y	Y	Y	Y	Y	M
Inspector, tester, sorter, sampler, and weigher	Y	Y	N	N	N	N	Y	N	N	N	Y	N	M
Jeweler and precious stone and metal worker	Y	N	N	Y	Y	Y	Y	N	N	N	Y	Y	H
Medical, dental, and ophthalmic laboratory technician	Y	N	Y	N	Y	Y	Y	N	Y	N	N	Y	M

Table A.17—Continued

Occupation	Easy to Get	Grew 2010–2018	Projected 2018–2028	All Workers	Black Men	Black Women	Hispanic Men	Hispanic Women	White Men	White Women	Other Men	Other Women	OJT
Packaging and filling machine operator and tender	Y	Y	Y	N	N	N	N	N	N	N	N	N	M
Painting worker and dyer	Y	Y	Y	N	Y	Y	Y	N	N	N	N	Y	M
Photographic process worker and processing machine operator	Y	N	N	N	Y	Y	N	Y	Y	N	Y	Y	L
Adhesive bonding machine operator and tender	Y	Y	N	N	Y	Y	Y	Y	N	Y	Y	Y	M
Cleaning, washing, and metal pickling equipment operator and tender	Y	N	Y	N	N	Y	Y	Y	N	Y	Y	Y	M
Etcher, engraver, and lithographer	Y	Y	Y	Y	Y	Y	Y	Y	N	Y	Y	Y	M
Molder, shaper, and caster, except metal and plastic	Y	Y	Y	N	Y	Y	N	Y	N	Y	N	Y	H

Table A.17—Continued

Occupation	Easy to Get	Grew 2010–2018	Projected 2018–2028	All Workers	Black Men	Black Women	Hispanic Men	Hispanic Women	White Men	White Women	Other Men	Other Women	OJT
Paper goods machine setter, operator, and tender	Y	N	N	N	Y	Y	N	Y	Y	Y	Y	Y	M
Tire builder	Y	N	N	Y	Y	Y	Y	Y	Y	Y	Y	Y	M
Helper—production workers	Y	N	Y	N	N	Y	N	N	N	N	Y	Y	L
Other production worker including semiconductor processor and cooling and freezing equipment operator	Y	Y	Y	N	Y	N	N	N	N	N	Y	N	M

NOTES: 2010–2018 growth data and high-paying calculations derived from the CPS. Projected growth and rating of the amount of OJT is from the BLS EP. Y = yes; N = no. OJT options are none (blank), low ("L"), moderate ("M"), and high ("H"). High-paying is calculated as being above the median wage for subbaccalaureate workers, both overall ("All") and by race/ethnic-gender interaction. *Easy to get* is an indicator for an occupation not requiring prior experience—it is a true entry-level occupation.

[a] Sample was too small to perform subgroup wage analysis. Not all occupations were available for education analysis.

TABLE A.18

Transportation and Material Moving Occupations

Occupation	Easy to Get	Grew 2010–2018	Projected 2018–2028	All Workers	Black Men	Black Women	Hispanic Men	Hispanic Women	White Men	White Women	Other Men	Other Women	OJT
Supervisor of transportation and material moving workers	N	N	Y	Y	Y	Y	Y	Y	Y	Y	Y	Y	
Air traffic controller and airfield operations specialist	Y	N	Y	Y	Y	Y	Y	Y	Y	Y	Y	Y	H
Flight attendant and transportation worker and attendant	N	Y	Y	N	Y	N	Y	N	N	Y	Y	Y	L/M
Bus and ambulance driver and attendant	Y	Y	Y	N	Y	N	Y	Y	N	N	N	N	L/M
Driver/sales worker and truck driver	Y	Y	Y	N	Y	N	N	N	N	N	N	Y	L
Taxi driver and chauffeur	Y	Y	Y	N	N	N	Y	Y	N	N	N	N	L
Motor vehicle operator, all other	Y	Y	Y	N	N	N	N	Y	N	Y	N	Y	L

Table A.18—Continued

Occupation	Easy to Get	Grew 2010–2018	Projected 2018–2028	All Workers	Black Men	Black Women	Hispanic Men	Hispanic Women	White Men	White Women	Other Men	Other Women	OJT
Locomotive engineer and operator	N	N	N	Y	Y	Y	Y	Y	Y	Y	Y	Y	M
Railroad brake, signal, and switch operator[a,b]		N	Y	N									
Railroad conductor and yardmaster	Y	Y	N	Y	Y	N	Y	Y	Y	Y	Y	Y	M
Subway, streetcar, and other rail transportation worker	Y	Y	Y	Y	Y	Y	Y	Y	Y	Y	Y	Y	M
Sailor and marine oiler, and ship engineer	N	N	N	Y	Y	Y	Y	Y	N	Y	Y	Y	M
Ship and boat captain and operator	N	N	N	Y	Y	Y	Y	Y	Y	Y	Y	Y	
Parking lot attendant	Y	Y	Y	N	N	Y	N	Y	N	Y	N	Y	L
Automotive and watercraft service attendant	Y	Y	Y	N	N	N	N	Y	N	N	N	Y	L

Table A.18—Continued

Occupation	Easy to Get	Grew 2010–2018	Projected 2018–2028	All Workers	Black Men	Black Women	Hispanic Men	Hispanic Women	White Men	White Women	Other Men	Other Women	OJT
Transportation inspector	Y	N	Y	Y	Y	Y	Y	Y	Y	Y	Y	Y	M
Transportation worker, not elsewhere classified	Y	Y	Y	Y	Y	Y	Y	Y	Y	Y	Y	Y	L/M
Crane and tower operator	N	Y	Y	Y	Y	Y	Y	Y	Y	Y	N	Y	M
Dredge, excavating, and loading machine operator	N	N	Y	Y	Y	Y	Y	Y	Y	Y	Y	Y	L/M
Conveyor operator and tender, and hoist and winch operator	Y	N	N	Y	Y	Y	Y	Y	Y	Y	Y	Y	L
Industrial truck and tractor operator	Y	Y	Y	N	N	N	N	Y	N	N	N	Y	L
Cleaner of vehicles and equipment	Y	Y	Y	N	N	N	N	N	N	N	N	N	L
Laborer and freight, stock, and material mover, hand	Y	Y	Y	N	N	N	N	N	N	N	N	N	L

Table A.18—Continued

Occupation	Easy to Get	Grew 2010–2018	Projected 2018–2028	All Workers	Black Men	Black Women	Hispanic Men	Hispanic Women	White Men	White Women	Other Men	Other Women	OJT
Transportation inspector	Y	N	Y	Y	Y	Y	Y	Y	Y	Y	Y	Y	M
Transportation worker, not elsewhere classified	Y	Y	Y	Y	Y	Y	Y	Y	Y	Y	Y	Y	L/M
Crane and tower operator	N	Y	Y	Y	Y	Y	Y	Y	Y	Y	N	Y	M
Dredge, excavating, and loading machine operator	N	N	Y	Y	Y	Y	Y	Y	Y	Y	Y	Y	L/M
Conveyor operator and tender, and hoist and winch operator	Y	N	N	Y	Y	Y	Y	Y	Y	Y	Y	Y	L
Industrial truck and tractor operator	Y	Y	Y	N	N	N	N	Y	N	N	N	Y	L
Cleaner of vehicles and equipment	Y	Y	Y	N	N	N	N	N	N	N	N	N	L
Laborer and freight, stock, and material mover, hand	Y	Y	Y	N	N	N	N	N	N	N	N	N	L

Table A.18—Continued

Occupation	Easy to Get	Grew 2010–2018	Projected 2018–2028	All Workers	Black Men	Black Women	Hispanic Men	Hispanic Women	White Men	White Women	Other Men	Other Women	OJT
Machine feeder and offbearer	Y	Y	Y	N	Y	N	N	N	N	N	Y	Y	L
Packer and packager, hand	Y	Y	N	N	N	N	N	N	N	N	N	N	L
Pumping station operator	N	Y	Y	Y	Y	Y	Y	Y	Y	Y	Y	Y	M
Refuse and recyclable material collector	Y	Y	Y	N	N	N	N	Y	N	Y	N	Y	L
Material moving worker, not elsewhere classified	Y	N	Y	N	Y	N	N	Y	N	Y	N	Y	L

NOTES: 2010–2018 growth data and high-paying calculations derived from the CPS. Projected growth and rating of the amount of OJT is from the BLS EP. Y = yes; N = no. OJT options are none (blank), low ("L"), moderate ("M"), and high ("H"). High-paying is calculated as being above the median wage for subbaccalaureate workers, both overall ("All") and by race/ethnic-gender interaction. *Easy to get* is an indicator for an occupation not requiring prior experience—it is a true entry-level occupation.

[a] Sample was too small to perform subgroup wage analysis.

[b] Not all occupations were available for education analysis.

APPENDIX B

Regional Variation

Our goal occupations are selected to help identify broad skill investments for the ChalleNGe program. Hence, we include as part of our assessment that jobs in those occupations should be widely available in different regions and localities in the United States. We define *widely available* to mean having a location quotient of at least 0.75. A *location quotient* is a measure of the concentration of jobs in an area relative to the overall concentration of jobs in the United States. So a quotient of at least 0.75 signifies that the number of employed persons in that occupation as a ratio of the population in a given region is not less than three-quarters of what it is in the United States overall. There are several candidate occupations that are not widely available in at least five regions of the United States.

Table B.1 lists the 11 subbaccalaureate occupations with the least broad availability across U.S. regions. They are concentrated in the construction, repair, and technician occupation families. Note that these occupation families have additional goal occupations that *do* have broad availability across U.S. regions; thus, we are unconcerned that the skill assessments may be too narrowly focused for some regions.

In contrast, there were occupation families that we dismissed entirely because the vast majority of their occupations had low availability in several regions. One example of this is the extraction occupation family. While extraction occupations meet the criteria of growing, in-demand occupations with a sustainable career path, they are too narrowly available to recommend for a national program. Moreover, many of the skills required by these occupations are also required for construction occupations, so cadets can develop the cross-applicable skills without specializing in an area unavailable to them.

TABLE B.1

Goal Occupations with Low Availability in at Least Five (of Nine) U.S. Regions

Occupation Family	Occupation
Construction	Drywall installer, ceiling tile installer, and taper
Engineering, science, and technician	Geological and petroleum technician
Office and administrative support	Communications equipment operator, all other
Construction	Plasterer and stucco mason
Engineering, science, and technician	Agricultural and food science technician
Arts and entertainment	Broadcast and sound engineering technician and radio operator, and media and communication equipment worker, all other
Protective services	Fire inspector
Construction	Boilermaker
Construction	Rail-track laying and maintenance equipment operator
Installation, maintenance, and repair	Aircraft mechanic and service technician
Installation, maintenance, and repair	Automotive glass installer and repairer

NOTE: *Low availability* is defined as a regional location quotient (employment-to-population ratio relative to the United States overall) of less than 0.75. Location quotient data are from the BLS's state-level Occupational Employment and Wage Statistics in 2018 (BLS, 2018).

The location quotient analysis also allows us to examine the overall variation by region (census division)—which regions have the broadest array of goal occupations available, and which have the fewest. The New England region (Connecticut, Maine, Massachusetts, New Hampshire, Rhode Island, and Vermont) has the fewest available, with just 60 out of a possible 97 occupations meeting our goal occupations criteria considered widely available. In contrast, the West South Central region (Arkansas, Louisiana, Oklahoma, and Texas) is missing only 11 occupations.

In Table B.2, we list all of the goal occupations along with an indicator for their availability in each region.

TABLE B.2

Goal Occupations, by Regional Availability

Occupation	East North Central	East South Central	Middle Atlantic	Mountain	New England	Pacific	South Atlantic	West North Central	West South Central
Claims adjuster, appraiser, examiner, and investigator	Y	Y	Y	Y	Y	Y	Y	Y	Y
Tax preparer	Y	Y	Y	Y	Y	Y	Y	Y	Y
Web developer	Y	N	Y	Y	Y	Y	Y	Y	N
Computer support specialist	Y	N	Y	Y	Y	Y	Y	Y	Y
Drafter	Y	Y	Y	Y	Y	Y	Y	Y	Y
Engineering technician, except drafter	Y	Y	N	Y	Y	Y	Y	Y	Y
Surveying and mapping technician	N	Y	N	Y	N	Y	Y	N	Y
Agricultural and food science technician	Y	N	N	N	N	Y	N	Y	Y
Chemical technician	Y	Y	Y	Y	Y	N	N	Y	Y
Geological and petroleum technician	N	N	N	Y	N	Y	N	N	Y
Miscellaneous life, physical, and social science technician	Y	N	Y	Y	N	Y	Y	N	Y

Table B.2—Continued

Occupation	East North Central	East South Central	Middle Atlantic	Mountain	New England	Pacific	South Atlantic	West North Central	West South Central
Paralegal and legal assistant	Y	N	Y	Y	Y	Y	Y	Y	Y
Miscellaneous legal support worker	N	N	Y	Y	N	Y	Y	Y	Y
Broadcast and sound engineering technician and radio operator, and media and communication equipment worker, all other	N	N	Y	Y	N	Y	Y	N	N
Radiation therapist	Y	Y	Y	N	Y	N	Y	Y	Y
Respiratory therapist	Y	Y	Y	Y	Y	Y	Y	Y	Y
Clinical laboratory technologist and technician	Y	Y	Y	Y	Y	Y	Y	Y	Y
Dental hygienist	Y	Y	Y	Y	Y	Y	Y	Y	Y
Diagnostic-related technologist and technician	Y	Y	Y	Y	Y	Y	Y	Y	Y
Emergency medical technician and paramedic	Y	Y	Y	Y	Y	N	Y	Y	Y
Health diagnosing and treating practitioner support technician	Y	Y	Y	Y	Y	Y	Y	Y	Y

Table B.2—Continued

Occupation	East North Central	East South Central	Middle Atlantic	Mountain	New England	Pacific	South Atlantic	West North Central	West South Central
Billing and posting clerk and machine operator	Y	Y	Y	Y	Y	Y	Y	Y	Y
Gaming cage worker	N	Y	N	Y		Y	N	Y	Y
Financial clerk, all other	N	Y	Y	Y	Y	Y	Y	Y	N
Brokerage clerk	Y	Y	Y	Y	Y	Y	Y	Y	Y
Court, municipal, and license clerk	Y	Y	N	Y	Y	Y	Y	Y	Y
Eligibility interviewer, government programs	N	Y	Y	Y	Y	Y	N	Y	Y
Interviewer, except eligibility and loan	Y	Y	Y	Y	Y	Y	Y	Y	N
Loan interviewer and clerk	Y	Y	N	Y	N	Y	Y	Y	Y
Reservation and transportation ticket agent and travel clerk	N	N	Y	Y	N	Y	Y	N	Y
Information and record clerk, all other	N	Y	N	Y	N	Y	Y	N	Y
Cargo and freight agent	Y	Y	Y	N	N	Y	Y	Y	Y
Courier and messenger	Y	Y	Y	Y	Y	Y	Y	N	Y

Table B.2—Continued

Occupation	East North Central	East South Central	Middle Atlantic	Mountain	New England	Pacific	South Atlantic	West North Central	West South Central
Licensed Practical and Licensed Vocational Nurse	Y	Y	Y	N	Y	N	Y	Y	Y
Medical records and health information technician	Y	Y	Y	Y	Y	Y	Y	Y	Y
Optician, dispensing	Y	Y	Y	Y	Y	Y	Y	Y	Y
Miscellaneous health technologist and technician	Y	N	Y	Y	Y	Y	Y	N	Y
Occupational therapist assistant and aide	Y	Y	Y	Y	Y	N	Y	Y	Y
Physical therapist assistant and aide	Y	Y	Y	Y	Y	N	Y	Y	Y
Firefighter	Y	Y	N	Y	Y	Y	Y	Y	Y
Fire inspector	N	Y	Y	N	N	N	Y	N	Y
Detective and criminal investigator	N	N	Y	Y	N	Y	Y	N	Y
Police officer	Y	Y	Y	Y	Y	Y	Y	Y	Y
Animal control worker	Y	Y	Y	Y	Y	Y	Y	N	Y
Communications equipment operator, all other	N	Y	Y	Y	N	N	N	N	N

Table B.2—Continued

Occupation	East North Central	East South Central	Middle Atlantic	Mountain	New England	Pacific	South Atlantic	West North Central	West South Central
Dispatcher	Y	Y	Y	Y	Y	Y	Y	Y	Y
Production, planning, and expediting clerk	Y	Y	Y	N	Y	Y	Y	Y	Y
Insurance claims and policy processing clerk	Y	N	Y	N	Y	Y	Y	Y	Y
Boilermaker	Y	Y	N	Y	N	N	N	N	Y
Brickmason, blockmason, and stonemason	Y	Y	Y	Y	Y	N	Y	Y	N
Carpenter	Y	N	Y	Y	Y	Y	Y	Y	N
Carpet, floor, and tile installer and finisher	Y	N	Y	Y	N	Y	Y	Y	N
Cement mason, concrete finisher, and terrazzo worker	Y	N	N	Y	N	Y	Y	Y	Y
Paving, surfacing, and tamping equipment operator	Y	Y	N	Y	N	N	Y	Y	Y
Construction equipment operator, except paving, surfacing, and tamping equipment operator	Y	Y	Y	Y	N	Y	Y	Y	Y

Table B.2—Continued

Occupation	East North Central	East South Central	Middle Atlantic	Mountain	New England	Pacific	South Atlantic	West North Central	West South Central
Drywall installer, ceiling tile installer, and taper	N	N	N	Y	N	Y	N	N	N
Electrician	Y	Y	Y	Y	Y	Y	Y	Y	Y
Glazier	Y	N	N	Y	N	Y	Y	Y	Y
Insulation worker	N	Y	N	Y	N	N	Y	Y	Y
Painter, construction and maintenance, and paperhanger	Y	N	Y	Y	Y	Y	Y	Y	Y
Pipelayer, plumber, pipefitter, and steamfitter	Y	Y	Y	Y	Y	Y	Y	Y	Y
Plasterer and stucco mason	N	N	N	Y	N	Y	N	N	Y
Reinforcing iron and rebar worker	N	Y	Y	Y	N	Y	Y	N	Y
Roofer	Y	N	N	Y	N	Y	Y	Y	N
Sheet metal worker	Y	Y	N	Y	Y	Y	Y	Y	Y
Structural iron and steel worker	Y	Y	Y	Y	Y	Y	N	Y	Y
Construction and building inspector	N	N	Y	Y	Y	Y	Y	N	Y

Regional Variation

Table B.2—Continued

Occupation	East North Central	East South Central	Middle Atlantic	Mountain	New England	Pacific	South Atlantic	West North Central	West South Central
Elevator installer and repairer	N	N	Y	N	Y	N	Y	Y	Y
Fence erector	N	N	N	Y	Y	Y	Y	Y	Y
Hazardous materials removal worker	Y	N	Y	Y	Y	Y	Y	N	Y
Highway maintenance worker	Y	Y	Y	Y	Y	Y	N	Y	Y
Rail-track laying and maintenance equipment operator	N	N	Y	N	Y	N	N	Y	Y
Avionics technician	N	Y	N	Y	N	Y	Y	Y	Y
Electric motor, power tool, and related repairer	Y	Y	N	Y	N	Y	Y	Y	Y
Electrical and electronics repairer, transportation equipment, industrial and utility	Y	Y	Y	Y	N	Y	Y	Y	Y
Security and fire alarm systems installer	N	Y	Y	Y	Y	Y	Y	Y	Y
Aircraft mechanic and service technician	N	N	N	Y	N	Y	Y	N	Y
Automotive body and related repairer	Y	Y	Y	Y	Y	Y	Y	Y	Y

Table B.2—Continued

Occupation	East North Central	East South Central	Middle Atlantic	Mountain	New England	Pacific	South Atlantic	West North Central	West South Central
Automotive glass installer and repairer	N	Y	N	N	Y	Y	N	N	Y
Automotive service technician and mechanic	Y	Y	Y	Y	Y	Y	Y	Y	Y
Bus and truck mechanic and diesel engine specialist	Y	Y	Y	Y	Y	Y	Y	Y	Y
Heavy vehicle and mobile equipment service technician and mechanic	Y	Y	N	Y	N	Y	Y	Y	Y
Small engine mechanic	Y	Y	Y	Y	Y	Y	Y	Y	Y
Control and valve installer and repairer	Y	Y	Y	Y	Y	N	Y	Y	Y
Heating, air conditioning, and refrigeration mechanic and installer	Y	Y	Y	Y	Y	N	Y	Y	Y
Home appliance repairer	Y	N	Y	Y	Y	Y	Y	Y	N
Industrial and refractory machinery mechanic	Y	Y	N	Y	N	N	Y	Y	Y
Maintenance and repair worker, general	Y	Y	Y	Y	Y	Y	Y	Y	Y

Table B.2—Continued

Occupation	East North Central	East South Central	Middle Atlantic	Mountain	New England	Pacific	South Atlantic	West North Central	West South Central
Maintenance worker, machinery	Y	Y	Y	Y	N	N	Y	Y	Y
Millwright	Y	Y	N	N	N	Y	Y	Y	Y
Electrical power-line installer and repairer	Y	Y	N	Y	Y	N	Y	Y	Y
Telecommunications line installer and repairer	N	N	Y	N	Y	Y	Y	Y	Y
Precision instrument and equipment repairer	Y	Y	Y	Y	N	Y	Y	Y	Y
Coin, vending, and amusement machine servicer and repairer	Y	Y	Y	Y	N	Y	N	Y	Y
Rigger	N	Y	N	N	Y	Y	Y	N	Y
Helper—installation, maintenance, and repair workers	N	Y	Y	Y	N	Y	Y	N	Y
Other installation, maintenance, and repair worker, including wind turbine service technician, commercial diver, and signal and train switch repairer	Y	Y	N	Y	N	Y	Y	Y	Y

NOTES: *Low availability* is defined as a regional location quotient (employment-to-population ratio relative to the United States overall) of less than 0.75. Location quotient data from the BLS's state-level Occupational Employment and Wage Statistics in 2018 (BLS, 2018).

Subgroups and Elements of O*NET Categories

In Chapter Five, we summarized O*NET elements that are ranked as important among the goal occupations. The majority of O*NET elements were not included; we present them here in Tables C.1 to C.5 and List C.1, organized by O*NET domain. Some domains, such as abilities, group elements by themes; we also list those here.

TABLE C.1

Abilities—Subgroups and Elements

Abilities			
Cognitive Abilities	**Physical Abilities**	**Psychomotor Abilities**	**Sensory Abilities**
Category flexibility	Dynamic flexibility	Arm-hand steadiness	Auditory attention
Deductive reasoning	Dynamic strength	Control precision	Depth perception
Flexibility of closure	Explosive strength	Finger dexterity	Far vision
Fluency of ideas	Extent flexibility	Manual dexterity	Glare sensitivity
Inductive reasoning	Gross body coordination	Multilimb coordination	Hearing sensitivity
Information ordering	Gross body equilibrium	Rate control	Near vision
Mathematical reasoning	Stamina	Reaction time	Night vision
Memorization	Static strength	Response orientation	Peripheral vision
Number facility	Trunk strength	Speed of limb movement	Sound localization
Oral comprehension		Wrist-finger speed	Speech clarity
Oral expression			Speech recognition
Originality			Visual color discrimination
Perceptual speed			
Problem sensitivity			
Selective attention			
Spatial orientation			
Speed of closure			
Time sharing			
Visualization			

Table C.1—Continued

Abilities			
Cognitive Abilities	Physical Abilities	Psychomotor Abilities	Sensory Abilities
Written comprehension			
Written expression			

TABLE C.2

Knowledge—Subgroups and Elements

Knowledge	
No Subgroups	
Administration and management	History and archeology
Biology	Law and government
Building and construction	Mathematics
Chemistry	Mechanical
Clerical	Medicine and dentistry
Communications and media	Personnel and human resources
Computers and electronics	Philosophy and theology
Customer and personal service	Physics
Design	Production and processing
Economics and accounting	Psychology
Education and training	Public safety and security
Engineering and technology	Sales and marketing
English language	Sociology and anthropology
Fine arts	Telecommunications
Food production	Therapy and counseling
Foreign language	Transportation
Geography	

TABLE C.3
Skills—Subgroups and Elements

Skills			
Basic Skills	**Resource Management Skills**	**Social Skills**	**Technical Skills**
Active learning	Management of financial resources	Coordination	Equipment maintenance
Active listening	Management of material resources	Instructing	Equipment selection
Critical thinking	Management of personnel resources	Negotiation	Installation
Learning strategies	Time management	Persuasion	Operation and control
Mathematics		Service orientation	Operation monitoring
Monitoring		Social perceptiveness	Operations analysis
Reading comprehension			Programming
Science			Quality control analysis
Speaking			Repairing
Writing			Technology design
			Troubleshooting
	Complex Problem-Solving Skills	**System Skills**	
	Complex problem solving	Judgment and decision making	
		System analysis	
		System evaluation	

TABLE C.4

Work Activities—Subgroups and Elements

Skills			
Information Input	**Interacting with Others**	**Mental Processes**	**Work Output**
Estimating the quantifiable of products, events, or information	Assisting and caring for others	Analyzing data or information	Controlling machines and processes
Getting information	Coaching and developing others	Developing objectives and strategies	Documenting/ recording information
Identifying objects, actions, and events	Communicating with persons outside organization	Evaluating information to determine compliance with standards	Drafting, laying out, and specifying technical devices, parts, and equipment
Inspecting equipment, structures, or material	Communicating with supervisors, peers, or subordinates	Judging the qualities of things, services, or people	Handling and moving objects
Monitoring processes, materials, or surroundings	Coordinating the work and activities of others	Making decisions and solving problems	Interacting with computers
	Developing and building teams	Organizing, planning, and prioritizing work	Operating vehicles, mechanized devices, or equipment
	Establishing and maintaining interpersonal relationships	Processing information	Performing general physical activities
	Guiding, directing, and motivating subordinates	Scheduling work and activities	Repairing and maintaining electronic equipment
	Interpreting the meaning of information for others	Thinking creatively	Repairing and maintaining mechanical equipment

Table C.4—Continued

	Skill		
Information Input	Interacting with Others	Mental Processes	Work Output
	Monitoring and controlling resources	Updating and using relevant knowledge	
	Performing for or working directly with the public		
	Providing consultation and advice for others		
	Resolving conflicts and negotiating with others		
	Selling and influencing others		
	Staffing organizational units		
	Training and teaching others		

TABLE C.5

Work Context—Subgroups and Elements

Interpersonal Relationships	Physical Work Conditions	Structural Job Characteristics
Contact with others	Cramped work space, awkward positions	Consequence of error
Coordinate or lead others	Exposed to contaminants	Degree of automation
Deal with external customers	Exposed to disease or infections	Duration of typical work week
Deal with physically aggressive people	Exposed to hazardous conditions	Freedom to make decisions
Deal with unpleasant or angry people	Exposed to hazardous equipment	Frequency of decision making
Electronic mail	Exposed to high places	Impact of decisions on coworkers or company results
Face-to-face discussions	Exposed to minor burns, cuts, bites, or stings	Importance of being exact or accurate
Frequency of conflict scenarios	Exposed to radiation	Importance of repeating same tasks
Letters and memos	Exposed to whole body vibration	Level of competition
Public speaking	Extremely bright or inadequate lighting	Pace determined by speed of equipment
Responsibility	In an enclosed vehicle or equipment	Structured versus unstructured work
Responsible for others' health and safety	In an open vehicle or equipment	Time pressure
Telephone	Indoors, environmentally controlled	Work schedules
Work with work group or team	Indoors, not environmentally controlled	
	Outdoors, exposed to weather	
	Outdoors, under cover	
	Physical proximity	

Table C.5—Continued

Interpersonal Relationships	Physical Work Conditions	Structural Job Characteristics
	Sounds, noise levels are distracting or uncomfortable	
	Spend time bending or twisting the body	
	Spend time climbing ladders, scaffolds, or poles	
	Spend time keeping or regaining balance	
	Spend time kneeling, crouching, stooping, or crawling	
	Spend time making repetitive motions	
	Spend time sitting	
	Spend time standing	
	Spend time using your hands to handle, control, or feel objects, tools, or controls	
	Spend time walking and running	
	Very hot or cold temperatures	
	Wear common protective or safety equipment, such as safety shoes, glasses, gloves, hearing protection, hard hats, or life jackets	
	Wear specialized protective or safety equipment, such as breathing apparatus, safety harness, full protection suits, or radiation protection	

LIST C.1
Work Styles—Subgroups and Elements

Work Styles
No Subgroups
Achievement/effort
Adaptability/flexibility
Analytical thinking
Attention to detail
Concern for others
Cooperation
Dependability
Independence
Initiative
Innovation
Integrity
Leadership
Persistence
Self control
Social orientation
Stress tolerance

Abbreviations

BLS	Bureau of Labor Statistics
CPS	Current Population Survey
DoL	U.S. Department of Labor
EP	Employment Projections
GED	General Educational Development
KSAs	knowledge, skills, and abilities
LMI	labor market information
OJT	on-the-job training
O*NET	Occupational Information Network
OOH	*Occupational Outlook Handbook*
SOC	Standard Occupational Classification
TABE	Test of Adult Basic Education
WIGS	Workforce Information Grants to States
WIOA	Workforce Innovation and Opportunity Act
WLMI	workforce and labor market information

Bibliography

Albert, Kyle, "The Certification Earnings Premium: An Examination of Young Workers," *Social Science Research*, Vol. 63, 2017, pp. 138–149.

Annual Reports and Information Staff, Institute of Education Sciences, National Center for Education Statistics, "Annual Earnings by Educational Attainment," webpage, updated May 2020. As of May 7, 2020: https://nces.ed.gov/programs/coe/indicator_cba.asp

Armour, Philip, Richard V. Burkhauser, and Jeff Larrimore, "Using the Pareto Distribution to Improve Estimates of Topcoded Earnings," *Economic Inquiry*, Vol. 54, No. 2, 2016, pp. 1263–1273.

Autor, David H., *The Polarization of Job Opportunities in the U.S. Labor Market: Implications for Employment and Earnings*, Washington, D.C.: Center for American Progress and Hamilton Project, April 2010. As of August 16, 2021: https://economics.mit.edu/files/5554

Autor, David H., David Dorn, and Gordon H. Hanson, "The China Syndrome: Local Labor Market Effects of Import Competition in the United States," *American Economic Review*, Vol. 103, No. 6, October 2013, pp. 2121–2168.

Autor, David H., Frank Levy, and Richard J. Murnane, "The Skill Content of Recent Technological Change: An Empirical Exploration," *Quarterly Journal of Economics*, Vol. 118, No. 4, November 2003, pp. 1279–1333.

Bailey, Thomas, Norena Badway, and Patricia J. Gumport, *For-Profit Higher Education and Community Colleges*, New York: Community College Research Center, Teachers College, Columbia University, March 2001. As of August 16, 2021: https://ccrc.tc.columbia.edu/publications/for-profit-higher-education.html

Bailey, Thomas, Davis Jenkins, and Timothy Leinbach, *What We Know About Community College Low-Income and Minority Student Outcomes: Descriptive Statistics from National Surveys*, New York: Community College Research Center, Teachers College, Columbia University, January 2005.

Baird, Matthew, Robert Bozick, and Melanie Zaber, "Beyond Traditional Academic Degrees: The Labor Market Returns to Occupational Credentials in the United States," RAND Corporation and Brown University Education Working Paper Series, EdWorkingPaper No. 21-381, April 2021. As of June 21, 2021: https://edworkingpapers.com/sites/default/files/ai21-381.pdf

Baker, Marissa G., Trevor K. Peckham, and Noah S. Seixas, "Estimating the Burden of United States Workers Exposed to Infection or Disease: A Key Factor in Containing Risk of COVID-19 Infection," *PloS One*, Vol. 15, No. 4, 2020, article e0232452.

Baker, Rachel, Eric Bettinger, Brian Jacob, and Ioana Marinescu, "The Effect of Labor Market Information on Community Colleges Students' Major Choice," National Bureau of Economic Research, Working Paper No. 23333, April 2017.

Bakhshi, Hasan, Jonathan M. Downing, Michael A. Osborne, and Philippe Schneider, *The Future of Skills: Employment in 2030*, London: Pearson and Nesta, 2017.

"Beauty Schools Directory," webpage, undated. As of October 21, 2021: https://beautyschoolsdirectory.com/

"Best Jobs Without a Degree," database, *U.S. News and World Report*, 2018.

Bird, Kisha, Marcie Foster, and Evelyn Ganzglass, *New Opportunities to Improve Economic and Career Success for Low-Income Youth and Adults: Key Provisions of the Workforce Innovation and Opportunity Act (WIOA)*, Washington, D.C.: Center for Law and Social Policy, September 2014. As of August 16, 2021: https://www.clasp.org/sites/default/files/public/resources-and-publications/publication-1/KeyProvisionsofWIOA-Final.pdf

Blau, Francine D., and Lawrence M. Kahn, "Gender Differences in Pay," *Journal of Economic Perspectives*, Vol. 14, No. 4, 2000, pp. 75–99. As of August 16, 2021: https://ideas.repec.org/a/aea/jecper/v14y2000i4p75-99.html

BLS—*See* U.S. Bureau of Labor Statistics.

Borghans, Lex, Bas ter Weel, and Bruce A. Weinberg, "Interpersonal Styles and Labor Market Outcomes," *Journal of Human Resources*, Vol. 43, No. 4, 2008, pp. 815–858.

Bosler, Canyon, and Nicolas Petrosky-Nadeau, "Job-to-Job Transitions in an Evolving Labor Market," *FRBSF Economic Letter*, Federal Reserve Bank of San Francisco, 2016-34, November 14, 2016. As of August 16, 2021: https://www.frbsf.org/economic research/files/el2016-34.pdf

Burrus, Jeremy, Teresa Jackson, Nuo Xi, and Jonathan Steinberg, *Identifying the Most Important 21st Century Workforce Competencies: An Analysis of the Occupational Information Network (O*NET)*, Princeton, N.J.: Educational Testing Service, Research Report ETS RR–13-21, November 2013. As of August 16, 2021: https://onlinelibrary.wiley.com/doi/pdf/10.1002/j.2333-8504.2013.tb02328.x

Card, David, and John E. DiNardo, "Skill-Biased Technological Change and Rising Wage Inequality: Some Problems and Puzzles," *Journal of Labor Economics*, Vol. 20, No. 4, 2002, pp. 733–783. As of August 16, 2021: http://davidcard.berkeley.edu/papers/skill-tech-change.pdf

Carnevale, Anthony P., Nicole Smith, and Jeff Strohl, *Help Wanted: Projections of Jobs and Education Requirements Through 2018*, Washington, D.C.: Georgetown University, Center on Education and the Workforce, June 2010.

Carnevale, Anthony P., Jeff Strohl, Neil Ridley, and Artem Gulish, *Three Educational Pathways to Good Jobs: High School, Middle Skills, and Bachelor's Degree*, Washington, D.C.: Georgetown University, Center on Education and the Workforce, 2018. As of August 16, 2021: https://cew.georgetown.edu/wp-content/uploads/3ways-FR.pdf

Cellini, Stephanie Riegg, "Financial Aid and For-Profit Colleges: Does Aid Encourage Entry?" *Journal of Policy Analysis and Management*, Vol. 29, No. 3, 2010, pp. 526–552.

Cellini, Stephanie Riegg, and Latika Chaudhary, "The Labor Market Returns to a For-Profit College Education," *Economics of Education Review*, Vol. 43, December 2014, pp. 125–140. As of August 16, 2021: https://doi.org/10.1016/j.econedurev.2014.10.001

Center for Global Policy Solutions, *Stick Shift: Autonomous Vehicles, Driving Jobs, and the Future of Work*, Washington, D.C., March 2017.

Cifuentes, Manuel, Jon Boyer, David A. Lombardi, and Laura Punnett, "Use of O*NET as a Job Exposure Matrix: A Literature Review," *American Journal of Industrial Medicine*, Vol. 53, 2010, pp. 898–914. As of August 16, 2021: https://onlinelibrary.wiley.com/doi/pdf/10.1002/ajim.20846

"College Tuition Compare," webpage, undated. As of October 21, 2021: https://collegetuitioncompare.com

Competency Model Clearinghouse, Career OneStop, "Develop a Career Ladder/Lattice," webpage, undated. As of October 21, 2021: https://www.careeronestop.org/competencymodel/getstarted/userguide_cll.aspx

Constant, Louay, Jennie W. Wenger, Linda Cottrell, Stephani L. Wrabel, and Wing Yi Chan, *National Guard Youth ChalleNGe: Program Progress in 2018–2019*, Santa Monica, Calif.: RAND Corporation, RR-4294-OSD, 2020. As of September 21, 2021: https://www.rand.org/pubs/research_reports/RR4294.html

Cooper, Preston, "Clipping Student Debt at Cosmetology Schools," *Forbes*, February 15, 2017. As of August 16, 2021: https://www.forbes.com/sites/prestoncooper2/2017/02/15/clipping-student-debt-at-cosmetology-schools/#5111ddf623cf

Council on Integrity in Results Reporting, "Real Data from Schools Committed to Transparency: Simple, Complete, and Comparable Outcomes Reports, Publicly Available," database, undated. As of August 16, 2021: https://cirr.org/data

"Credential Finder," webpage, undated. As of June 21, 2021: https://credentialfinder.org/

Daly, Mary C., Bart Hobijn, and Joseph H. Pedtke, "Disappointing Facts About the Black-White Wage Gap," *FRBSF Economic Letter*, Federal Reserve Bank of San Francisco, 2017-26, September 5, 2017. As of August 16, 2021: https://www.frbsf.org/economic-research/publications/economic-letter/2017/september/disappointing-facts-about-black-white-wage-gap/

Deming, David, Claudia Goldin, and Lawrence F. Katz, "The For-Profit Postsecondary School Sector: Nimble Critters or Agile Predators?" New York: Center for Analysis of Postsecondary Education and Employment, February 2012. As of August 16, 2021: https://capseecenter.org/for-profit-nimble-critters/

DoL—*See* U.S. Department of Labor.

Gittleman, Maury, Mark A. Klee, and Morris M. Kleiner, "Analyzing the Labor Market Outcomes of Occupational Licensing," *Industrial Relations: A Journal of Economy and Society*, Vol. 57, No. 1, January 2018, pp. 57–100.

Global Data, *Project Insight—Construction in Key USA States*, London, June 2019. As of August 16, 2021: https://store.globaldata.com/report/gdcn0056wp--project-insight-construction-in-key-us-states/?utm_source=email&utm_medium=pr&utm_campaign=190701a_gd_ct_pr_construction_US_states&utm_nooveride=1

Gould, Elise, "State of Working America Wages 2018: Wage Inequality Marches On—and Is Even Threatening Data Reliability," Washington, D.C.: Economic Policy Institute, February 20, 2019. As of August 16, 2021: https://www.epi.org/publication/state-of-american-wages-2018/

Gould, Elise, "Black-White Wage Gaps Are Worse Today Than in 2000," *Working Economics Blog*, Economic Policy Institute, February 27, 2020. As of August 16, 2021: https://www.epi.org/blog/black-white-wage-gaps-are-worse-today-than-in-2000/

Graf, Nikki, Anna Brown, and Eileen Patten, "The U.S. Gender Pay Gap Is Narrowing but Persistent," Washington, D.C.: Pew Research Center, April 12, 2018.

Green, Andrew, "What Is Happening to Middle Skill Workers?" *OECD Social, Employment, and Migration Working Papers*, No. 230, June 2019. As of August 16, 2021: https://www.oecd-ilibrary.org/docserver/a934f8fa-en.pdf

Jenkins, Davis, and Christopher Spence, *The Career Pathways How-To Guide*, Workforce Strategy Center, October 2006. As of August 16, 2021: https://files.eric.ed.gov/fulltext/ED496995.pdf

Jovicic, Sonja, "Wage Inequality, Skill Inequality, and Employment: Evidence and Policy Lessons from PIAAC," *IZA Journal of European Labor Studies*, Vol. 5, No. 21, 2016.

Kleiner, Morris M., and Alan B. Krueger, "Analyzing the Extent and Influence of Occupational Licensing on the Labor Market," *Journal of Labor Economics*, Vol. 31, No. 2, April 2013, pp. S173–S202.

Kochan, Thomas A., David Finegold, and Paul Osterman, "Who Can Fix the 'Middle-Skills' Gap?" *Harvard Business Review*, December 2012. As of August 16, 2021: https://hbr.org/2012/12/who-can-fix-the-middle-skills-gap

Kofi Charles, Kerwin, Erik Hurst, and Mariel Schwartz, "The Transformation of Manufacturing and the Decline in U.S Employment," in Martin Eichenbaum and Jonathan A. Parker, eds., *NBER Macroeconomics Annual 2018*, Vol. 33, Chicago: University of Chicago Press, June 2019, pp. 307–372. As of August 16, 2021: https://www.nber.org/chapters/c14081

Kolodner, Meredith, and Sarah Butrymowicz, "A $21,000 Cosmetology School Debt, and a $9-an-Hour Job," *New York Times*, December 26, 2018.

Labor Market Information Unit, Tennessee Department of Labor and Workforce Development, *The Construction Workforce in Davidson County and the Local Workforce Development Area*, Nashville, Tenn., undated. As of August 19, 2021: https://www.jobs4tn.gov/admin/gsipub/htmlarea/uploads/LMI/Publications/Construction_in_Davidson_County_and_LWDA.pdf

Levy, Frank, and Richard J. Murnane, *The New Division of Labor: How Computers Are Creating the Next Job Market*, Princeton, N.J.: Princeton University Press, 2004.

Liu, Vivian Yuen Ting, and Clive Belfield, *Evaluating For-Profit Higher Education: Evidence from the Education Longitudinal Study*, New York: Community College Research Center, Teachers College, Columbia University, 2014a. As of August 16, 2021: https://ccrc.tc.columbia.edu/publications/evaluating-for-profit-higher-education-els.html

Handel, Michael J., "The O*NET Content Model: Strengths and Limitations: Stärken und Grenzen des O*NET-Models," *Journal for Labour Market Research*, Vol. 49, 2016, pp. 157–176. As of August 16, 2021: https://link.springer.com/article/10.1007/s12651-016-0199-8

Harvard Business School, "Bridge the Gap: Rebuilding America's Middle Skills," 2014. As of December 20, 2021: https://www.hbs.edu/competitiveness/research/Pages/research-details. aspx?rid=66

Hegewisch, Ariane, and Zohal Barsi, *The Gender Wage Gap by Occupation 2019*, Washington, D.C.: Institute for Women's Policy Research, March 2020. As of October 28, 2021: https://iwpr.org/iwpr-issues/employment-and-earnings/ the-gender-wage-gap-by-occupation-2019/

Heywood, John S., and Xiangdong Wei, "Education and Signaling: Evidence from a Highly Competitive Labor Market," *Education Economics*, Vol. 12, No. 1, 2004, pp. 1–16.

"Highest Paying Jobs Without a Degree," database, *U.S. News and World Report*, 2018.

High School District 214 (Illinois), "Career Clusters and Pathways," webpage, 2019. As of August 19, 2021: https://www.discover214.org/career-pathway-terminology-and-definitions-2

Holzer, Harry J., "Raising Job Quality and Skills for American Workers: Creating More-Effective Education and Workforce Development Systems in the States," Washington, D.C.: Brookings Institution and Hamilton Project, 2011-10, November 2011.

Holzer, Harry J., and Robert I. Lerman, *America's Forgotten Middle-Skill Jobs: Education and Training Requirements for the Next Decade and Beyond*, Washington, D.C.: Skills 2 Compete, November 2007.

Horrigan, Michael W., "Employment Projections to 2012: Concepts and Context," *Monthly Labor Review*, February 2004, pp. 3–22.

Huang, Jason L., and Marina Pearce, "The Other Side of the Coin: Vocational Interests, Interest Differentiation and Annual Income at the Occupation Level of Analysis," *Journal of Vocational Behavior*, Vol. 83, 2013, pp. 315–326. As of August 16, 2021: http://www.jasonhuangatwork.com/papers/ Huang_&_Pearce_2013_JVB-interest&income.pdf

Hughes, Katherine L. , and Melinda Mechur Karp, *Strengthening Transitions by Encouraging Career Pathways: A Look at State Policies and Practices*, New York: Community College Research Center, Teachers College, Columbia University, January 2006.

Liu, Vivian Yuen Ting, and Clive Belfield, *The Labor Market Returns to For-Profit Higher Education: Evidence for Transfer Students*, New York: Community College Research Center, Teachers College, Columbia University, November 2014b. As of August 16, 2021:
https://ccrc.tc.columbia.edu/publications/
labor-market-returns-to-for-profit-higher-education.html

Lund, Susan, James Manyika, Liz Hilton Segel, André Dua, Bryan Hancock, Scott Rutherford, and Brent Macon, *The Future of Work in America: People and Places, Today and Tomorrow*, New York: McKinsey & Company, July 2019. As of August 16, 2021:
https://www.mckinsey.com/featured-insights/future-of-work/
the-future-of-work-in-america-people-and-places-today-and-tomorrow

Maguire, Sheila, Joshua Freely, Carol Clymer, Maureen Conway, and Deena Schwartz, *Tuning in to Local Labor Markets: Findings from the Sectoral Employment Impact Study*, Philadelphia, Pa.: Public/Private Ventures, 2010. As of August 16, 2021:
https://ppv.issuelab.org/resources/5101/5101.pdf

Marinescu, Ioana, and Roland Rathelot, "The Geography of Job Search and Mismatch Unemployment," Job Market Paper, Paris School of Economics, November 6, 2013. As of August 16, 2021:
https://www.parisschoolofeconomics.eu/IMG/pdf/
marinescu-pse-rues-janv2014.pdf

Maryland Department of Labor, "Spotlight: Cybersecurity, Labor Market Information for Maryland Job Seekers and Businesses," fact sheet, June 2017. As of August 16, 2021:
https://mwejobs.maryland.gov/admin/gsipub/htmlarea/uploads/
SpotlightCybersecurity_newLMI.pdf

Mishel, Lawrence, Heidi Shierholz, and John Schmitt, *Don't Blame the Robots: Assessing the Job Polarization Explanation of Growing Wage Inequality*, Washington, D.C.: Economic Policy Institute, November 19, 2013. As of August 19, 2021:
https://www.epi.org/publication/
technology-inequality-dont-blame-the-robots/

Modestino, Alicia Sasser, "The Importance of Middle-Skill Jobs," *Issues in Science and Technology*, National Academy of Sciences, Vol. 33, No. 1, 2016. As of August 16, 2021:
https://issues.org/the-importance-of-middle-skill-jobs/

Moscarini, Giuseppe, and Francis G. Vella, "Occupational Mobility and the Business Cycle," National Bureau of Economic Research, Working Paper 13819, February 2008. As of August 16, 2021:
https://www.nber.org/papers/w13819

Mumford, Troy V., Michael A. Campion, and Frederick P. Morgeson, "A Leadership Skills Strataplex: Leadership Skill Requirements Across Organizational Levels," *Academy of Management Proceedings*, Vol. 2003, No. 1, December 2017. As of August 16, 2021: https://journals.aom.org/doi/pdf/10.5465/ambpp.2003.13792974

National Research Council, *Assessing 21st Century Skills: Summary of a Workshop*, Washington, D.C.: National Academies Press, 2011.

National Skills Coalition, "Lack of Access to Skills Training Hurts Workers and Businesses," fact sheet, undated-a. As of August 19, 2021: https://nationalskillscoalition.org/resources/publications/middle-skill-fact-sheets/file/US_skillsmismatch.pdf

National Skills Coalition, "United States' Forgotten Middle," fact sheet, undated-b.

Nolan, Christine, Ed Morrison, Indraneel Kumar, Hamilton Galloway, and Sam Cordes, "Linking Industry and Occupation Clusters in Regional Economic Development," *Economic Development Quarterly*, Vol. 25, No. 1, 2011, pp. 26–35. As of August 19, 2021: https://journals.sagepub.com/doi/pdf/10.1177/0891242410386781

Oesch, Daniel, and Giorgio Piccitto, "The Polarization Myth: Occupational Upgrading in Germany, Spain, Sweden, and the UK, 1992–2015," *Work and Occupations*, Vol. 46, No. 4, 2019, pp. 441–469.

Ohio Department of Education, "Career Pathways," webpage, undated. As of October 22, 2021: https://education.ohio.gov/Topics/Career-Tech/Career-Connections/Career-Pathways

O*NET, "Instructions for Making Work Style Ratings," O*NET Work Styles Questionnaire, undated. As of September 13, 2021: https://www.onetcenter.org/dl_files/MS_Word/Work_Styles.pdf

O*NET OnLine, "Abilities," webpage, undated-a. As of August 19, 2021: https://www.onetonline.org/find/descriptor/browse/Abilities/

O*NET OnLine, "Knowledge," webpage, undated-b. As of August 19, 2021: https://www.onetonline.org/find/descriptor/browse/Knowledge/

O*NET OnLine, "Skills," webpage, undated-c. As of August 19, 2021: https://www.onetonline.org/find/descriptor/browse/Skills/

O*NET OnLine, "Summary Report for: 39-5012.00–Hairdressers, Hairstylists, and Cosmetologists," webpage, undated-d. As of December 20, 2021: https://www.onetonline.org/link/summary/39-5012.00

O*NET OnLine, "Work Activities," webpage, undated-e. As of August 19, 2021: https://www.onetonline.org/find/descriptor/browse/Work_Activities/

O*NET OnLine, "Work Context," webpage, undated-f. As of August 19, 2021:
https://www.onetonline.org/find/descriptor/browse/Work_Context/

O*NET OnLine, "Work Styles," webpage, undated-g. As of August 19, 2021:
https://www.onetonline.org/find/descriptor/browse/Work_Styles/

O*Net OnLine, "Summary Report for 49-2097.00–Audiovisual Equipment Installers and Repairers," webpage, updated 2020. As of September 3, 2021:
https://www.onetonline.org/link/summary/49-2097.00

O*Net OnLine, "Summary Report for 27-4031.00–Camera Operators, Television, Video, and Film," webpage, updated 2021a. As of September 3, 2021:
https://www.onetonline.org/link/summary/27-4031.00

O*Net OnLine, "Summary Report for 31-1121.00–Home Health Aides," webpage, updated 2021b. As of September 3, 2021:
https://www.onetonline.org/link/summary/31-1121.00

O*Net OnLine, "Summary Report for 31-1122.00–Personal Care Aides," webpage, updated 2021c. As of September 3, 2021:
https://www.onetonline.org/link/summary/31-1122.00

O*Net OnLine, "Summary Report for: 31-2011.00–Occupational Therapy Assistants," updated 2021d. As of December 15, 2021:
https://www.onetonline.org/link/summary/31-2011.00

Passel, Jeffrey S., *Size and Characteristics of the Unauthorized Migrant Population in the U.S.: Estimates Based on the March 2005 Current Population Survey*, Washington, D.C.: Pew Hispanic Center, 2006.

Pellegrino, James W., and Margaret L. Hilton, eds., Committee on Defining Deeper Learning and 21st Century Skills; Board on Testing and Assessment; Board on Science Education; Division of Behavioral and Social Sciences and Education; and National Research Council, *Education for Life and Work: Developing Transferable Knowledge and Skills in the 21st Century*, Washington, D.C.: National Academies Press, 2012.

Poole, Kenneth E., Ronald Kelly, Lauren Gilchrist, and Andrew Reamer, *Labor Market Information Customers and Their Needs: Customer-Oriented LMI Product Innovation*, Arlington, Va.: LMI Training Institute, April 18, 2012. As of October 27, 2021:
https://www.lmiontheweb.org/wp-content/uploads/sites/4/2020/02/2012-05-08_-_LMI_Customers_and_Their_Needs.pdf

Public Law 73-30, Wagner-Peyser Act of 1933, June 6, 1933. As of September 7, 2021:
https://www.dol.gov/agencies/eta/american-job-centers/wagner-peyser

Public Law 105-220, Workforce Investment Act of 1998, August 7, 1998.

Rapacon, Stacy, "30 of the Best Jobs for the Future," Kiplinger, December 12, 2018. As of September 7, 2021:
https://www.kiplinger.com/slideshow/business/
T012-S001-best-jobs-for-the-future-2018/index.html

Redbird, Beth, "The New Closed Shop? The Economic and Structural Effects of Occupational Licensure," *American Sociological Review*, Vol. 82, No. 3, 2017, pp. 600–624.

Ricketts, Glenn, "Community Colleges: A Brief History," National Association of Scholars blog post, July 23, 2009. As of August 19, 2021:
https://www.nas.org/blogs/article/community_colleges_a_brief_history

Saavedra, Anna Rosefsky, and V. Darleen Opfer, "Learning 21st-Century Skills Requires 21st-Century Teaching," *Phi Delta Kappan*, Vol. 94, No. 2, October 2012, pp. 8–13. As of December 28, 2021:
https://journals.sagepub.com/doi/full/10.1177/003172171209400203

Salsberg, Edward, and Robert Martiniano, "Health Care Jobs Projected to Continue to Grow Far Faster Than Jobs in the General Economy," *Health Affairs* blog, May 9, 2018. As of August 19, 2021:
https://www.healthaffairs.org/do/10.1377/hblog20180502.984593/full/

Sloane, Peter J., "Overeducation, Skill Mismatches, and Labor Market Outcomes for College Graduates," *IZA World of Labor*, November 2014.

Stone, Robyn I., and Natasha S. Bryant, "The Future of the Home Care Workforce: Training and Supporting Aides as Members of Home-Based Care Teams," *Journal of the American Geriatrics Society*, Vol. 67, No. S2, 2019, pp. S444–S448.

U.S. Bureau of Labor Statistics, "Employment Projections," webpage, undated. As of August 23, 2021:
https://www.bls.gov/emp/

U.S. Bureau of Labor Statistics, "Occupational Employment and Wage Statistics," database, 2018. As of September 15, 2021:
https://www.bls.gov/oes/tables.htm

U.S. Bureau of Labor Statistics, "Barbers, Hairstylists, and Cosmetologists," webpage, updated April 10, 2020a. As of May 6, 2020:
https://www.bls.gov/ooh/personal-care-and-service/
barbers-hairstylists-and-cosmetologists.htm

U.S. Bureau of Labor Statistics, "Usual Weekly Earnings of Wage and Salary Workers: First Quarter 2020," press release, Washington, D.C., April 15, 2020b.

U.S. Bureau of Labor Statistics, *Occupational Outlook Handbook*, website, Washington, D.C., last updated April 9, 2021. As of September 3, 2021:
https://www.bls.gov/ooh/

U.S. Census Bureau, U.S. Bureau of Labor Statistics, "Current Population Survey," webpage, undated. As of August 23, 2021:
https://www.census.gov/programs-surveys/cps.html

U.S. Department of Labor Employment and Training Administration, *Labor Market Information: An Overview*, Washington, D.C., 1997.

U.S. Department of Labor, Employment and Training Administration, "Training and Employment Guidance Letter No. 15-10: Increasing Credential, Degree, and Certificate Attainment by Participants of the Public Workforce System," Washington, D.C., December 15, 2010. As of August 16, 2021:
https://wdr.doleta.gov/directives/attach/TEGL15-10.pdf

U.S. News and World Report, "Best Health Care Jobs," webpage, 2021a. As of December 14, 2021:
https://money.usnews.com/careers/best-jobs/rankings/best-healthcare-jobs

U.S. News and World Report, "Best Jobs Without a College Degree," webpage, 2021b. As of December 14, 2021:
https://money.usnews.com/careers/best-jobs/rankings/best-jobs-without-a-college-degree

U.S. News and World Report, "Highest Paying Jobs Without a Degree," webpage, 2021c. As of December 14, 2021:
https://money.usnews.com/careers/best-jobs/rankings/highest-paying-jobs-without-a-degree

Wagner, Tony, *The Global Achievement Gap: Why Even Our Best Schools Don't Teach the New Survival Skills Our Children Need—and What We Can Do About It*, New York: Basic Books, 2008.

Wenger, Jennie W., Louay Constant, and Linda Cottrell, *National Guard Youth ChalleNGe: Program Progress in 2016–2017*, Santa Monica, Calif.: RAND Corporation, RR-2276-OSD, 2018. As of August 19, 2021:
https://www.rand.org/pubs/research_reports/RR2276.html

The White House, "Fact Sheet: Biden Administration to Take Steps to Bolster Registered Apprenticeships," webpage, February 17, 2021. As of June 21, 2021:
https://www.whitehouse.gov/briefing-room/statements-releases/2021/02/17/fact-sheet-biden-administration-to-take-steps-to-bolster-registered-apprenticeships/

Zaber, Melanie A., Lynn A. Karoly, and Katie Whipkey, *Reimagining the Workforce Development and Employment System for the 21st Century and Beyond*, Santa Monica, Calif.: RAND Corporation, RR-2768-RC, 2019. As of August 19, 2021:
https://www.rand.org/pubs/research_reports/RR2768.html